¡Buen Viaje!

Jo Anne Wilson
Educational Consultant

Jacqueline Moase-Burke
Oakland Schools, Waterford, Michigan

Prentice
Hall

Glenview, Illinois
Needham, Massachusetts
Upper Saddle River, New Jersey

CREDITS

Publisher: Stanley J. Galek
Editorial Director: Janet Dracksdorf
Marketing Manager: Elaine Uzan Leary
Production Editor: Pamela Warren
Developmental Editor: Margaret Potter

Also participating in the publication of this text were:

Editorial Production Manager: Elizabeth Holthaus
Assistant Editor: Mary McKeon
Manufacturing Coordinator: Jerry Christopher
Interior Design: Imageset Design
Interior Layout and Composition: Johnny D'Ziner
Cover Design: Imageset Design
Illustrations: Robin Swennes, Imageset Design

PHOTOGRAPHS

Stuart Cohen: pages 35 (all), 39, 50 (all), 56 (all), 57 (all).
W.D. Morgan: pages 10, 12, 27 (all), 59, 122 (bottom right), 156 (left).
Margaret Potter: pages 122 (bottom left, bottom center), 156 (right).

ISBN 0-8384-4934-4

20 21 V003 12 11 10

DEDICATION

We dedicate this book to the special people in our lives, who have loved, supported, and encouraged us throughout this project:

- Vi Scharbat, Joe Scharbat and Sally Gorenflo, Ron Kramer and "Rudnicks"
- Mike Burke, the Moase family (Ken, Dale, Sue, Eric, Alex, Tina, Jacob, and Vanessa) and Myra Baughman

ACKNOWLEDGEMENTS

We would like to acknowledge and thank our colleagues, Ligia Bueno, Luis Delacruz, María Etienne, Giannina Villegas, who gave us their linguistic expertise.

REVIEWERS

In particular, we wish to thank the four teachers who reviewed our entire manuscript and gave us invaluable criticisms and suggestions.

Bob Abel
Roeper School
Bloomfield Hills, MI

Susan Malik
Swift Creek Middle School
Midlothian, VA

Yvette Parks
Norwood Public Schools
Norwood, MA

Patrick Raven
Foreign Language Department Chairman
School District of Waukesha
Waukesha, WI

CONTENTS

TO THE STUDENT   1

Apellido *Sullivan* Nombre *Kristina*
Dirección *36570 Utica Road*
Summerville, MI 48096 USA
Teléfono *313-296-4157*

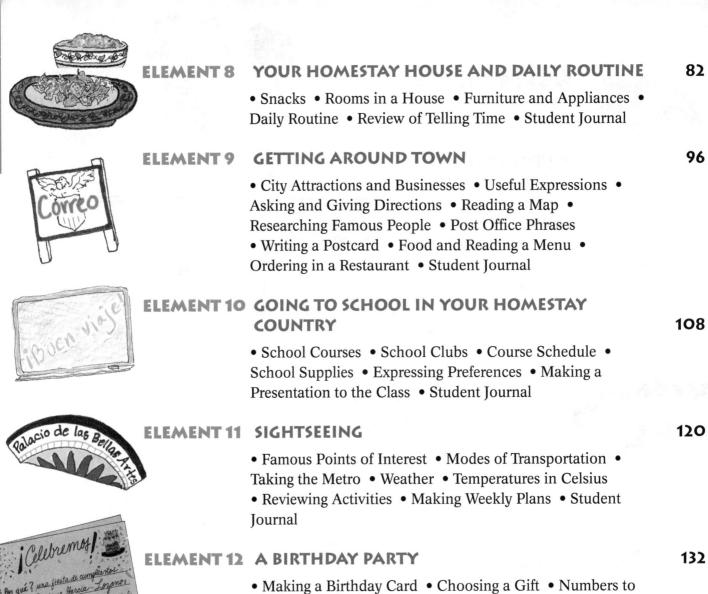

TO THE STUDENT

There are many languages in the world that people use to communicate with each other. In this book, you are about to explore one that is spoken in many parts of the world—SPANISH. You will learn not only some of the Spanish language itself, but also information about the people who speak it and the countries where they live.

The lessons in *¡Buen viaje!*, called Elements, take you through the steps you would follow if you were preparing for and participating in a homestay as an exchange student in a Spanish-speaking country. In fact, you will be working through these steps just as if you were really going! You will learn words and phrases that are important for communicating with the people you'll meet, and you will participate in activities that help you prepare for your trip and get the most out of your homestay experience when you get there.

As you begin, listen carefully to the sounds of the language. Then practice saying the words and phrases that you hear. Try them with your friends and family. Perhaps you can find an exchange student or someone in your community who speaks Spanish, and you can practice with him or her! You'll also have an opportunity to write in a journal, which will help you remember the language as you practice your writing skills. In addition, you'll have an opportunity to use drawings and pictures as visual cues for remembering words and phrases.

Exploring a language that is different from your own is like learning a special code, and it can even help you understand your own language better. Learning any language is a process that takes place over an extended period of time. This book offers you an opportunity to start that process. As you progress through the Elements, have fun and explore! We really hope you'll have a *¡Buen viaje!*

THE SPANISH-SPEAKING WORLD

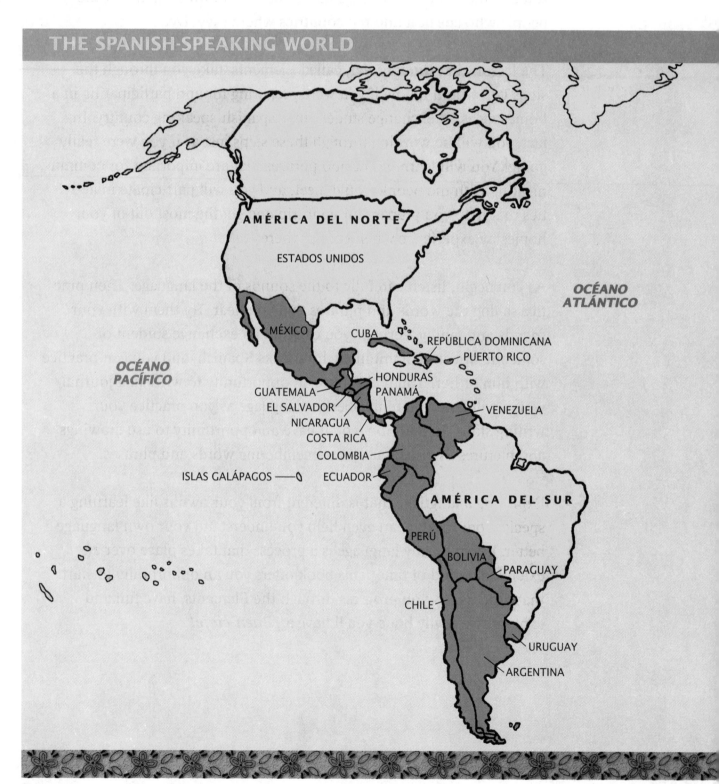

AMÉRICA DEL NORTE

ESTADOS UNIDOS

OCÉANO ATLÁNTICO

OCÉANO PACÍFICO

MÉXICO

CUBA

REPÚBLICA DOMINICANA

PUERTO RICO

HONDURAS

GUATEMALA

PANAMÁ

EL SALVADOR

VENEZUELA

NICARAGUA

COSTA RICA

COLOMBIA

ISLAS GALÁPAGOS

ECUADOR

AMÉRICA DEL SUR

PERÚ

BOLIVIA

PARAGUAY

CHILE

URUGUAY

ARGENTINA

Do you know that Spanish is the second most commonly spoken language in the United States? The map on this page shows the many countries around the world where Spanish is the official language. In this Element you are going to learn about Spanish-speaking countries. As you learn about these countries, think about one in particular that you would like to visit. Why? Because this year you are going to have the opportunity to be an exchange student. You are going on a homestay with a Spanish-speaking family!

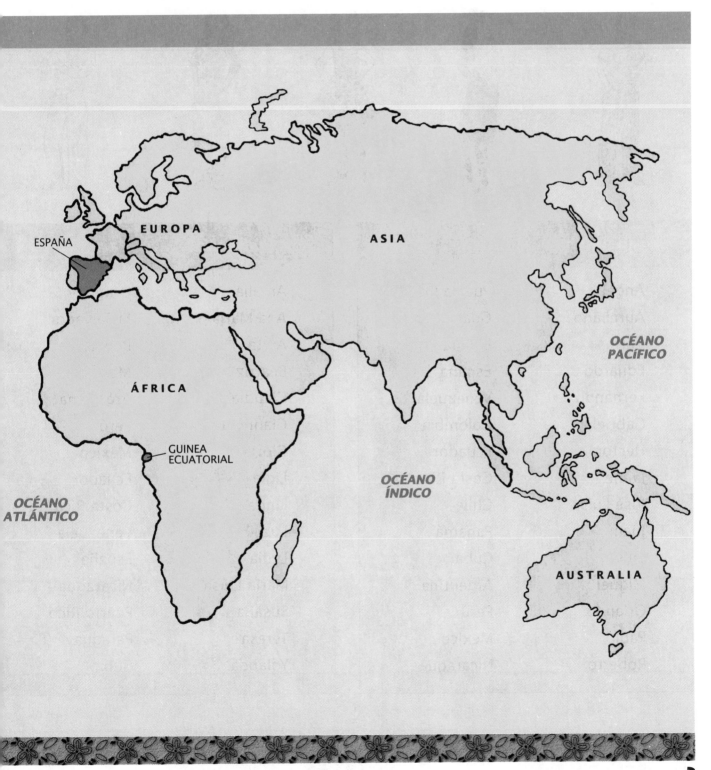

A. INTERNATIONAL YOUTH CONFERENCE

An international youth conference is taking place in your city. What a wonderful opportunity for you to meet young people from around the world! This is also a great time to get some first-hand information about a possible choice for your homestay country. At the conference, you decide to write down the names of all your new Spanish-speaking friends and their countries. Here are the lists you made. Find each country on your map of the world on pages 2–3.

Muchachos	País
Angel	Puerto Rico
Aureliano	Guatemala
Carlos	Bolivia
Eduardo	España
Fernando	Venezuela
Gabriel	Colombia
Héctor	Ecuador
Jaime	Costa Rica
José Luis	Chile
Juan	Panamá
Luis	Cuba
Miguel	Argentina
Orlando	Perú
Pablo	México
Roberto	Nicaragua

Muchachas	País
Amalia	Uruguay
Ana María	El Salvador
Anita	Bolivia
Beatriz	México
Claudia	Argentina
Giannina	Perú
Gloria	México
Ligia	Ecuador
Linda	Costa Rica
Luz	Venezuela
Lydia	España
María Luisa	Nicaragua
Susana	Puerto Rico
Teresa	Paraguay
Yolanda	Cuba

B. MEETING NEW FRIENDS

At the youth conference registration table, you see all the name tags in different languages. This is your chance to meet students from the countries you'll be considering for your homestay. It's also your opportunity to practice using Spanish to meet and greet someone. Look closely at the Spanish name tags below.

Buenos días

Me llamo _Eduardo_

Soy de _España_

International Youth Conference

Buenos días

Me llamo _María Luisa_

Soy de _Nicaragua_

International Youth Conference

Buenos días

Me llamo _Miguel_

Soy de _Argentina_

International Youth Conference

Read the name tags. Then write the appropriate answer in each blank.

1. Which word on the name tags means *Hello?* _____

2. **Me llamo** means _____

3. Which words on the name tags mean *I'm from?* _____

4. List the names of these three Spanish-speaking students. _____

   _____

5. There is one girl. What is her name? _____

6. List the names of the two boys. _____

7. List the three countries these students come from. _____

   _____

8. Locate these countries on your map.

9. Who lives in Central America? _____

Now you are going to use four new Spanish expressions—**Buenos días**, **Me llamo**, **Soy de**, and **Mucho gusto**—to meet and greet new Spanish-speaking friends. Your teacher will review these expressions with you and tell you what to do.

C. YOUTH AMBASSADOR

All students who go on homestays become youth ambassadors for their countries. On your home-stay you'll be an ambassador for the United States. You'll be able to share your view of American life with your homestay family and new friends. Because the United States is a large country composed of people from many backgrounds, not everyone will have the same views you have.

1. *Individually:* Think about what your life is like in the United States. Which important aspects of your life would you like to share with your homestay family and new friends? Write them in your suitcase of ambassador information.

2. *In small groups:* Now share your own ideas with a small group of classmates. Listen to the other students express their ideas. Talk about what you will tell your host families about these things. If you like any of your classmates' ideas, you may add them to your own suitcase of ambassador information.

Favorite Foods

_____

_____

_____

Favorite Pastimes

_____

_____

_____

Favorite Customs

_____

_____

_____

What's Important to Me

_____

_____

_____

I am Proud of . . .

_____

_____

_____

My Friends

_____

_____

_____

D. SPAIN

Here is a map of **España**, the country in Europe (see your map of the Spanish-speaking World) where the Spanish language was first spoken. Maybe Spain will be your homestay destination. Let's look at some geographical terms in Spanish.

A. How do Spanish-speaking students write the following?

1. Atlantic Ocean _____

   _____

2. Mediterranean Sea _____

   _____

3. Strait of Gibraltar _____

   _____

OCÉANO ATLÁNTICO
MAR CANTÁBRICO
FRANCIA
Santander Bilbao
Santiago Pirineos ANDORRA
Pamplona
Valladolid Río Ebro Gerona
Zaragoza Barcelona
Segovia
Salamanca MENORCA
La Sierra de ★ MADRID MALLORCA
Guadarrama Toledo
PORTUGAL Valencia
Río Tajo ESPAÑA IBIZA
Ciudad Real
Alicante
Córdoba Murcia
Sevilla Río Guadalquivir MAR MEDITERRÁNEO
Granada La Sierra Nevada
Cádiz Málaga
Estrecho de Gibraltar

B. Search the map to find the following information.

1. Circle three major mountainous regions on your map.

2. Name the river that flows through **Sevilla**. _____

3. Which very long river begins in Spain and runs through Portugal to the **Océano Atlántico**?

   _____

4. Which river empties into the **Mar Mediterráneo**? _____

5. Spain is bounded by _____ bodies of water. What do you think Spanish students do when

   they go on vacation to one of these coastal areas? _____

   _____

6. Look at the map. Listen while your teacher names some of the geographic points of interest discussed above. When you hear a location, place your finger on that area of the map. Your teacher will give you the correct answer after naming each location. How many did you get right? Try doing the same with a partner.

E. CITIES IN SPAIN

Here are some important cities in Spain (**ciudades en España**). The homestay family you select may live in one of them. The first letter of the name of each city is on the map. Use the list below to complete the names on the map.

Madrid	Valencia	Santiago	Córdoba	Zaragoza	Valladolid
Sevilla	Pamplona	Barcelona	Granada	Ciudad Real	Toledo

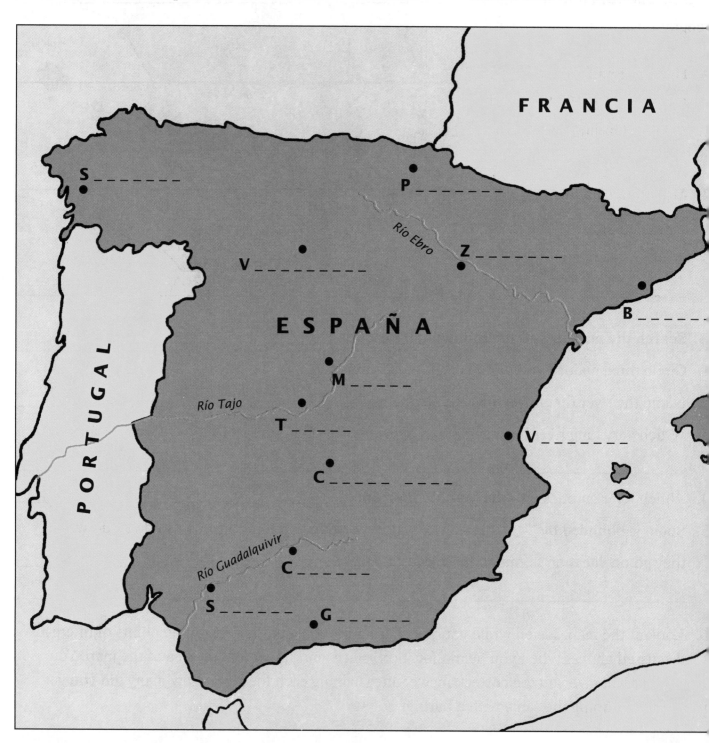

F. MEXICO, CENTRAL AMERICA, AND THE CARIBBEAN

You might consider a home-stay a little closer to home than Spain. Here is a map of **México**, **América Central**, and **el Caribe** (see your map of the Spanish-speaking World). Let's look at some more geographical terms in Spanish. These can be very useful in planning your visit.

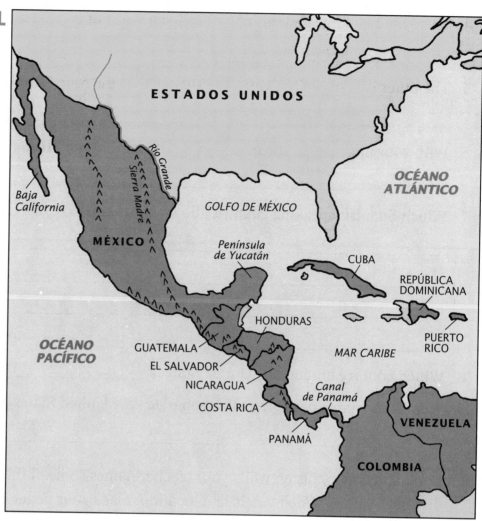

A.   How do Spanish-speaking students write the following?

1. Pacific Ocean _____

2. Atlantic Ocean _____

3. Gulf of Mexico _____

4. Caribbean Sea _____

B.   Search the map to find the following information.

1. Circle the major mountainous regions on your map.

2. Name the canal that connects the **Océano Pacífico** and the **Mar Caribe**. _____

   _____

3. Which Spanish-speaking island in the **Mar Caribe** is closest to Florida? _____

4. There are two large peninsulas in **México**. One is on the **Océano Pacífico**. Its name is

_____

5. The other is between the **Golfo de México** and the **Mar Caribe**. It's the _____

_____

6. With your finger, trace the mountains that run through **México**. What is the name of these

mountains?_____

7. Which Spanish-speaking countries lie south of Mexico? List them from north to south.

_____

_____

_____

_____

8. Which country borders the United States? _____

9. What is the name of the river that separates the United States and this country? _____

_____

10. Look at the map. Listen while your teacher names some of the geographic points of interest discussed above. When you hear a location, place your finger on that area of the map. Your teacher will give you the correct answer after naming each location. How many did you get right? Try doing the same with a partner.

Chapultepec Park, Mexico City

G. SOUTH AMERICA

Since you live in North America, wouldn't it be fun to spend your homestay in South America (**América del Sur**)? There are so many countries where Spanish is spoken. You really have a lot of choices. Look at the map of South America. Here are some additional geographical terms in Spanish.

A. How do Spanish-speaking students write the following?

1. Pacific Ocean _____

2. Atlantic Ocean _____

3. Gulf of Mexico _____

4. Caribbean Sea _____

B. Search the map to find the following information.

1. Circle the major mountainous region on your map.

2. Name the river that flows through **Venezuela**._____

3. Which river begins in **Perú** and **Colombia** and runs to **Brasil**?_____

_____

4. Which rivers empty into the **Océano Atlántico**? _____

_____

5. Which countries in South America do not border on water?_____

_____

_____

6. With your finger, trace the mountains that run through South America. What is the name of

these mountains? _____

List the seven countries where the mountains are located._____

_____

_____

_____

7. Where do you think the weather is hottest in July? _____

_____

Where do you think it is hottest in December? _____

_____

8. Look at the map. Listen while your teacher names some of the geographic points of interest
   discussed above. When you hear a location, place your finger on that area of the map. Your
   teacher will give you the correct answer after naming each location. How many did you get
   right? Try doing the same with a partner.

Quito, Ecuador

H. RECOGNIZING COUNTRIES AND CONTINENTS

You have learned about Spanish-speaking countries around the world. Referring to your map on pages 2–3, review these countries. Find the continent where each country is located and write the letter code for that continent in the blank.

América del Norte = **N**   América del Sur = **S**   África = **A**   Europa = **E**

Note: In this activity, Central American countries are considered to be part of South America. Caribbean countries are considered to be part of North America.)

____ 1. Guatemala   ____ 4. Bolivia   ____ 7. Guinea Ecuatorial   ____ 10. Argentina

____ 2. España   ____ 5. México   ____ 8. Nicaragua   ____ 11. El Salvador

____ 3. Venezuela   ____ 6. Panamá   ____ 9. Puerto Rico   ____ 12. Colombia

I. SPANISH WORDS YOU KNOW: COGNATES

You've learned a bit about the countries where Spanish is spoken. Now you really need to focus on the language you'll be using. Spanish is an exciting and interesting language. There are many Spanish words that look like English words but are pronounced differently. These words, called *cognates*, may be spelled the same in both languages or a little differently. Here is a list of Spanish words that last year's homestay students wrote for you. Let's see how many you know!

THINGS AND PEOPLE

el animal	la catedral	el fútbol	la nación	el rodeo
el arte	el chile	la hamburguesa	el papá	la salsa
el autobús	el chocolate	la historia	el parque	el sándwich
la avenida	la ciencia	el hóspital	el parque zoológico	el taco
el banco	la coca cola	el hotel	el piano	el taxi
el básquetbol	la comunicación	la malteada	la pizza	la televisión
el béisbol	el dólar	la mamá	el policía	el tenis
la bicicleta	la familia	el menú	el océano	el tomate
la blusa	la física	el monumento	el radio	el video
el café	la fruta	la música	el restaurante	el volibol

DESCRIPTIONS

africano	colorado	inteligente	privado	violeta
americano	importante	negro	público	

J. COGNATE CATEGORIES

Did you know a lot of the words in the list of cognates? Can you think of any others? Sort the words in the list into the following categories.

1. Sports

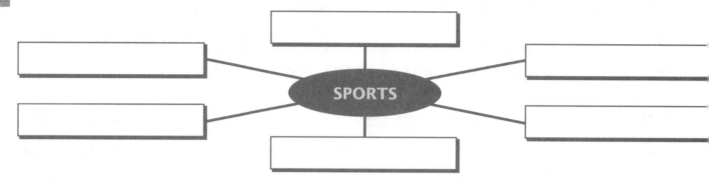

2. Food and drink

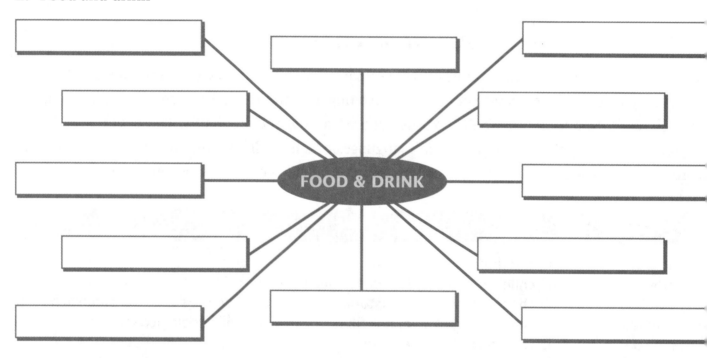

3. Modes of transportation _____

_____

4. Colors _____

5. Create a category name in English for the following words on the list: **el arte**, **la biología**, **la ciencia**, **la historia**, **la física**. _____

_____

X. MY JOURNAL

You're ready to choose your homestay country. It was helpful meeting students who live in these countries, wasn't it? You are going to keep a journal about your plans and your homestay. Select five to ten new Spanish words you need to remember. Write those words in your journal under the heading **Mis palabras**, which means *My words*. Also in your journal include any new information about the country and city you researched. Write this information under **Información nueva**, which means *New information*. Draw the flag and/or a map of your country under **Mi dibujo**, which means *My drawing*.

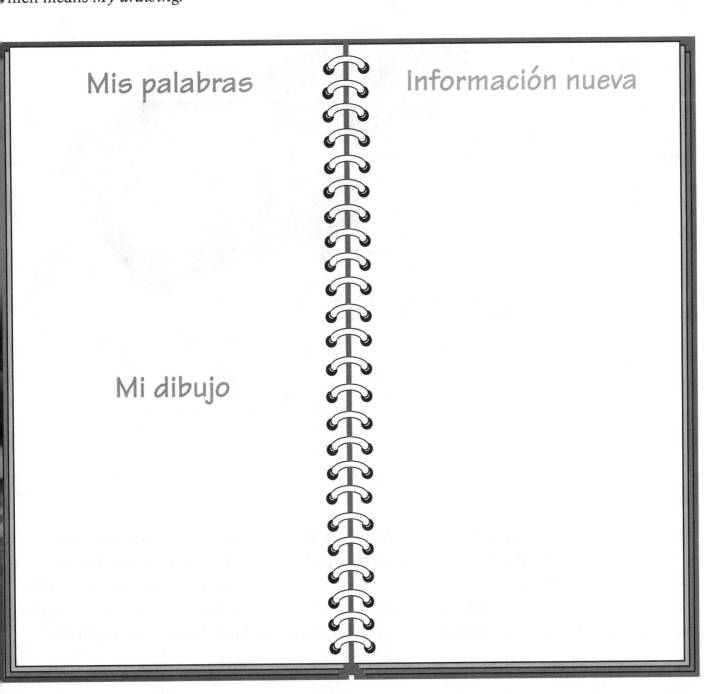

Mis palabras

Información nueva

Mi dibujo

2 PACKING

PERSPECTIVA

Look at the picture of
the suitcase to the right.
What do you think you'll
be learning in this Element?
Can you guess what the
Spanish words mean?
How will learning about
these things help you
plan for your homestay?

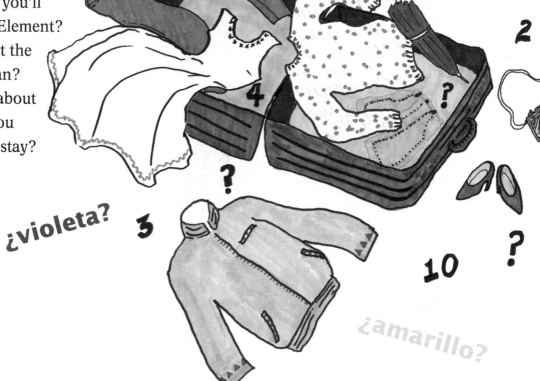

¿verde? 1 ? 8 ? ¿rosada?

9

2

¿violeta? 3

10 ?

¿amarillo?

A. CLOTHING

By now you've selected a country for your homestay. It's never too early to think about the
clothing you'll take on your trip. You want to have plenty of time to plan what you'll wear and to
see if it will fit in your suitcase. Below are pictures of clothing and travel items you may want to
pack for your trip. Listen carefully while your teacher says the words in Spanish. Notice that the
name of each item has another word in front of it. Both **el** and **la** are Spanish words for *the*.

In Spanish, you almost always include the equivalent of *the* when referring to the names of things. If you are talking about more than one, you use **los** (for **el** words) or **las** (for **la** words). They all mean *the*. Different, isn't it? But, with a little practice, you'll remember. To practice, look at the pictures again, and say the Spanish words with your teacher or a partner.

la camiseta

los jeans

los calcetines

la falda

el vestido

el par de zapatos

el cinturón

la peinilla

el reloj

el paraguas

los pantalones cortos

el cepillo

la sudadera

el cepillo de dientes

la blusa

la camisa

el suéter

la mochila

los pantalones

la chaqueta

la pasta de dientes

Now, use the webs below to sort the items on page 17. This will help you remember when to use **el**, **la**, **los** (you don't need **las** in this activity).

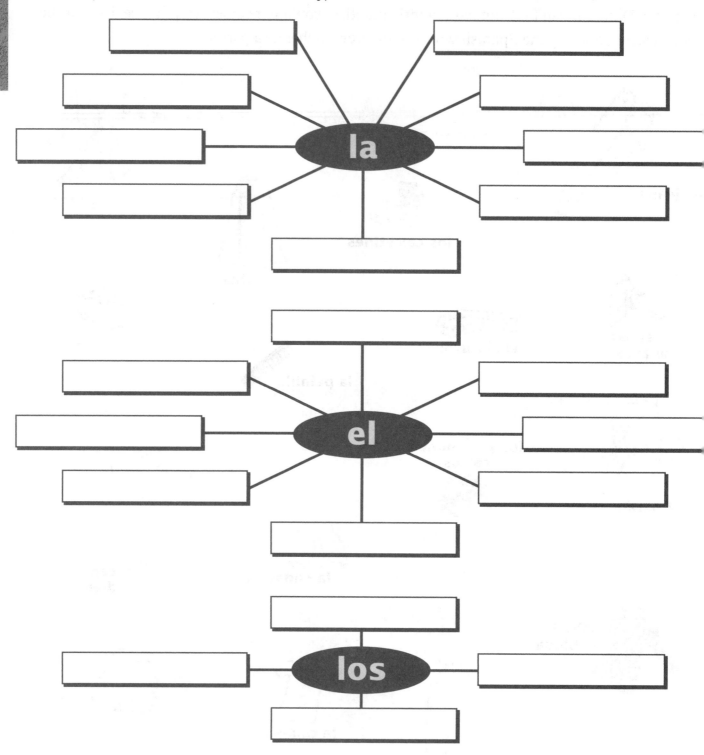

These words will be very helpful if you decide to do some shopping in your homestay country. Wouldn't it be great to buy a sweatshirt while you're there? Now you know exactly what to ask for in Spanish.

B. NUMBERS

There are many reasons to learn Spanish numbers (**los números**). You'll use numbers often during your homestay. Look at Spanish words for the numbers from 1 to 10. Count with your teacher.

| 1 | **uno** | 3 | **tres** | 5 | **cinco** | 7 | **siete** | 9 | **nueve** |
| 2 | **dos** | 4 | **cuatro** | 6 | **seis** | 8 | **ocho** | 10 | **diez** |

1 2 3 4 5 6 7 8 9 10

C. PACKING PRACTICE

You've learned the names of some clothing and travel items in Spanish. On page 20 is a drawing of a large empty suitcase. Use this empty suitcase to practice packing. You'll need pictures from old magazines and catalogs or from the hand-out your teacher gives you. Or you may want to draw your own items. Follow these steps:

1. Cut out—or draw and cut out—pictures of clothing and travel items.
2. On the back of each item write its Spanish name.
3. Place the pictures on your desk so you can see all of them.
4. Listen as your teacher says the name of an item.
5. Place the picture of the item in your suitcase as you quietly repeat the name to yourself.
6. Check your progress with your teacher.

With a partner, take turns packing your suitcase.

1. Partner A names an item in Spanish.
2. Partner B repeats the name of the item and places the picture of the item in the suitcase.
3. Partner A checks to see if partner B packed the right thing.
4. When the suitcase is packed, change roles.
5. When you're sure you know the Spanish names for all the items, paste the pictures in the suitcase.
6. Finally, label the pictures carefully in Spanish.

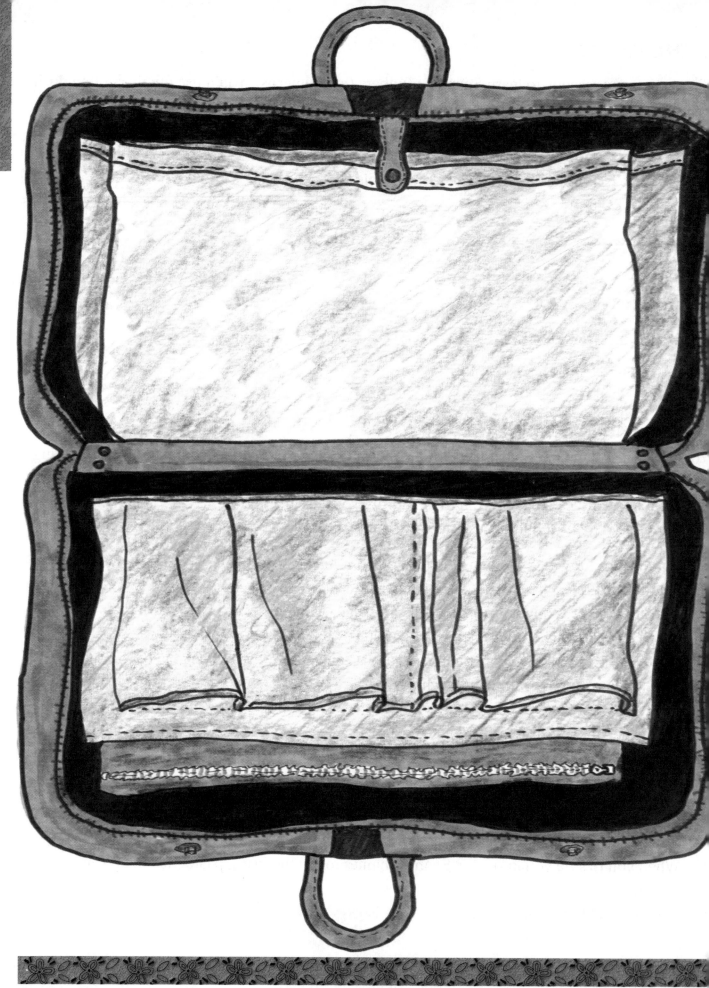

D. HOW MANY ARE YOU TAKING?

A good way to practice Spanish numbers is by talking about how many items you plan to pack for your homestay. You want to have enough of everything to last for the whole trip. Below is a list of some clothing and travel items you may need. Notice that there is an **s** on the end of some of the words. Both Spanish and English add **s** (and sometimes **es**) when talking about more than one of an item. Follow these steps:

1. Listen as your teacher reads each item and quantity in Spanish.
2. Write the corresponding numeral in the first blank after the item.
3. Check your answers as your teacher reads the numbers back to you.
4. Make any necessary corrections.
5. Finally, practice writing the Spanish words for the numerals. Look at the numeral in the first blank. Write the word in Spanish for that numeral in the blank on the right as you quietly repeat the number to yourself.

Example:

   camisas   *8*   *ocho*

1. jeans   _____   _____

2. camisetas   _____   _____

3. pares de zapatos   _____   _____

4. pantalones   _____   _____

5. suéter   _____   _____

6. vestidos   _____   _____

7. calcetines   _____   _____

8. faldas   _____   _____

9. camisas   _____   _____

10. peinillas   _____   _____

E. COLORS

What clothes to wear! How many clothes to take? You want to look terrific! What colors will be best? There are many reasons to learn the colors (**los colores**). If you decide to buy some clothes in your homestay country, you'll need to know how to ask for the colors you want. Look at the sweaters above and listen as your teacher says their colors in Spanish. Then practice with a partner. In Spanish, Partner A says the number of a sweater. Partner B then says the color of the sweater in Spanish. When all the colors have been named, switch roles.

F. THE SUITCASE

In Activity A, you learned different ways Spanish speakers say *the.* They also use different forms of many adjectives (words that are used to describe people and things). This happens, for example with colors. Look at the color words below. To know which form to use, take your cue from the Spanish word for *the.* For some color words there are two choices. For others there is only one.

LOS COLORES

azul

verde

rojo   roja

negro   negra

blanco   blanca

amarillo   amarilla

anaranjado   anaranjada

rosado   rosada

violeta

marrón

f there is only one choice, it is used with both **el** and **la**. When there are two choices, it works as follows:

- "**el**" words use the "**o**" form of the color.
- "**la**" words use the "**a**" form of the color.

Here are examples of how you use the correct color word to describe an article of clothing.

Examples: **el** suéter roj**o**   **la** falda roj**a**

The suitcase (**la maleta**) below has been divided into two compartments, one labeled **EL** and one **LA**. Articles of clothing have been placed in the appropriate compartments. This makes it easy for you to select the correct form of the color word when there are two choices. If an item is in the **EL** compartment, choose the form of the color that ends with **o**. If the item is in the **LA** compartment, choose the form ending in **a**. If there is only one form of the color, it's easy—one form can be used for both! Choose a color for each item in the suitcase by writing the correct form of the color in the blank. Be sure to use each color at least once!

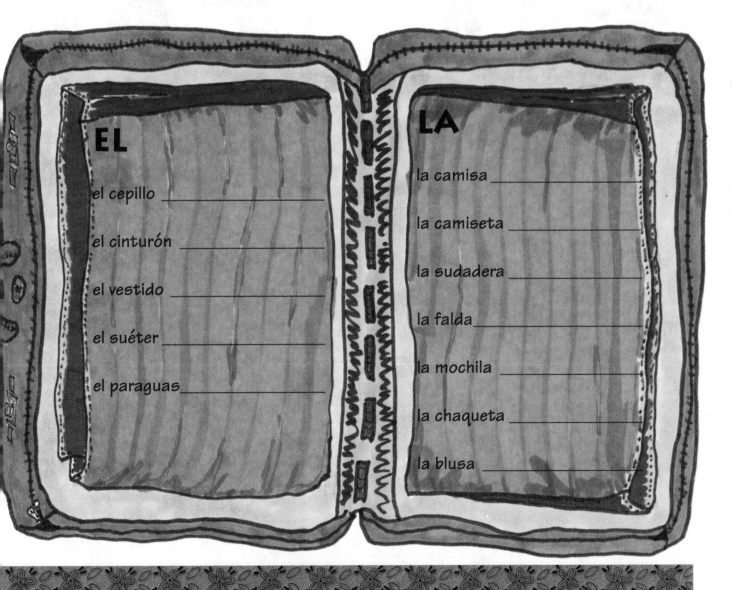

EL

el cepillo _____

el cinturón _____

el vestido _____

el suéter _____

el paraguas_____

LA

la camisa _____

la camiseta _____

la sudadera _____

la falda_____

la mochila _____

la chaqueta _____

la blusa _____

G. PACKING FOR YOUR TRIP

You have a lot of clothes, but you can take only a few. Here's a sample packing list. It names articles of clothing and travel items and their colors. Circle the picture that corresponds to the description in the packing list.

In Activity D you learned that both Spanish and English add **s** (and sometimes **es**) to mean that there is more than one of an item. In the list below, you'll see that some *colors* have an added **s** or **es** because they describe more than one of an item. **¡Buena suerte!**

PACKING LIST

1. jeans azules

2. camiseta blanca

3. chaqueta verde

4. calcetines blancos

5. camisa roja

6. par de zapatos marrones

7. suéter violeta

8. pantalones negros

9. peinilla rosada

13. mochila azul

0. cepillo marrón

14. cepillo de dientes verde

11. vestido amarillo

15. falda anaranjada

12. sudadera anaranjada

16. paraguas rojo

Would you pack some things that aren't on the list? To find out how to say them in Spanish, ask your teacher or look in a dictionary. Then write them here.

_____ _____ _____

_____ _____ _____

_____ _____ _____

H. MY JOURNAL

The airline allows you to take two pieces of luggage. You decide to take a suitcase (**maleta**) and your backpack (**la mochila**). You'll check **la maleta** at the gate, but you'll keep **la mochila** with you. What will you put in your **maleta** and what will you put in your **mochila**? (Remember to pack the most necessary items in **la mochila** in case the airline loses your suitcase.) In your journal, make a list of the items you need to take on your homestay. Decide how many and what colors of each item you'll need to pack. Then write each item on the journal page titled either **Maleta** or **Mochila** depending on where you'll pack it. Don't forget to use **el**, **la**, **los**, or **las** and the correct form of the color word.

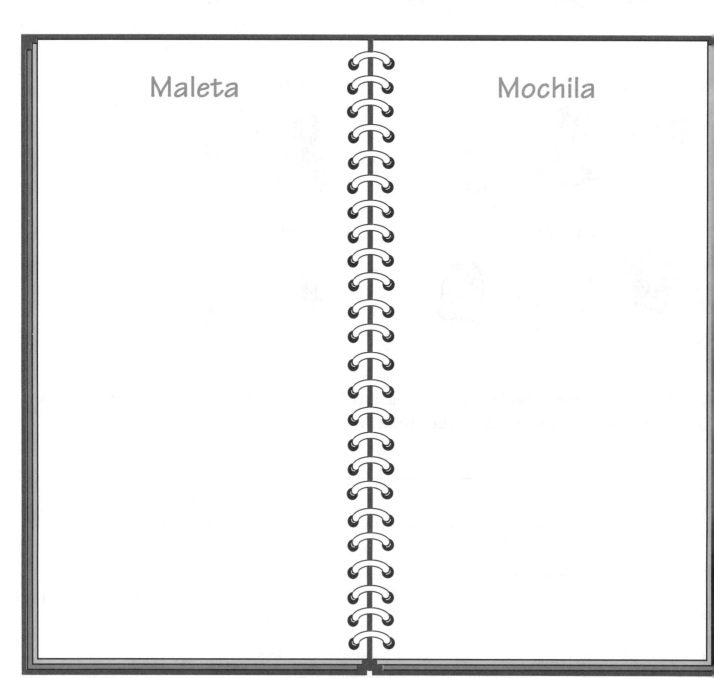

Maleta

Mochila

ELEMENT

Mexico City

Cañaris Indians, Ecuador

Woman weaving, Peru

3 TRIP PLANS

PERSPECTIVA

You've chosen your homestay
country and decided what to
pack in your suitcase. Now it's
time to make some other plans for
your trip. What else do you need?
One extremely important item that you'll
need is a passport! In this Element, you'll
fill out an application for a passport.
You'll also learn more numbers and how
to say the months, days, and dates you
need to schedule events.

A. MI AÑO ESCOLAR
(MY SCHOOL YEAR)

To participate in a successful homestay trip, students, parents, and teachers need to begin to plan
early. Homestay trips often take several months to organize. To plan your homestay adventure,
you need to learn some important phrases in Spanish.

An essential phrase for you to know is:

    ¿Cómo se dice _____ en español?   *How do you say _____ in Spanish?*

The answer to this question is usually:

    Se dice _____.   *You say _____.*

For example, if you don't know the word for *month* in Spanish, you will need to ask someone:
¿Como se dice *month* en español? The person will then answer: **Se dice *mes.***

Look at the months (**los meses**) written below. Circle any that you recognize. Many of them are cognates. (You learned about cognates in Element 1.) Read the months with your teacher. Here's the first page of a planning calendar for the school year (**el año escolar**). To practice spelling the months, write them where they belong in the calendar. Begin with the first month of your school year. Be careful. In Spanish, you do not capitalize the names of months.

mayo   octubre   marzo   septiembre   julio   diciembre
febrero   abril   noviembre   agosto   enero   junio

El año escolar

_____   _____

_____   _____

_____   _____

_____   _____

_____   _____

_____   _____

B. MI CUMPLEAÑOS (MY BIRTHDAY)

Now that you know the twelve months (**los doce meses**) of the year, you can identify the month of your birthday. *My birthday* in Spanish is **mi cumpleaños**. Look at the Spanish word for *birthday*. Do you recognize a part of the word? Ask your teacher if you guessed correctly. Write the **mes** of your **cumpleaños** here. _____

C. ENCUESTAS (SURVEYS)

Surveys are a good way to get information. To find out when your classmates and other people have birthdays, complete the following two **encuestas**. Then report your findings to the class. Remember to use only Spanish for these **encuestas**.

1. *Classmate tally.* Circulate around the room and ask all the students in the class, **¿Cuándo es tu cumpleaños?** (*When is your birthday?*). Each time a person answers, write his or her initials next to the month. You have ten minutes to get this information. Ready? (**¿Listos?**) Let's go! (**¡Vámonos!**)

¿Cuándo es tu cumpleaños?		
enero	mayo	septiembre
febrero	junio	octubre
marzo	julio	noviembre
abril	agosto	diciembre

Recording your data:

Which **mes** has the most **cumpleaños**? _____

Which **mes** has the fewest **cumpleaños**? _____

2. *Ask some others.* Find five people (friends, family members) to interview. Write their names in the boxes labeled **Nombre** (*Name*) below. Ask them when their birthday is. Write each person's birthday month in Spanish in the second column, next to his or her name.

Nombre	Cumpleaños
1.	
2.	
3.	
4.	
5.	

. LOS DÍAS DE LA SEMANA (DAYS OF THE WEEK)

ook at the blank calendar below. Write the name of the current month in the space at the top of
he calendar. To complete the calendar, what else do you need? You're right; you need days of the
eek and dates. **¿Cómo se dice** *day* **en español? Se dice** *día.*

most Spanish-speaking countries, the calendar week begins with Monday (**lunes**) and ends
ith the weekend, Saturday (**sábado**) and Sunday (**domingo**).

he days of the week (**Los días de la semana**) are not capitalized in Spanish. Practice saying the
ays of the week. Your teacher will get you started.

lunes   martes   miércoles   jueves   viernes   sábado   domingo

ook at the calendar again. In the seven spaces below the name of the month, fill in each **día de**
 semana. Remember to begin with **lunes** on the left.

E. LOS NÚMEROS (NUMBERS)

Knowing the months of the year and days of the week is important for your homestay preparations. Look again at the calendar in Activity D on page 31. You have already filled in the name of this month and the days of the week. To use the calendar, you need the dates. Complete the calendar on page 31 for the current month by beginning with 1 on the correct day of the week. You've already learned the numbers from 1 to 10. Count quietly to yourself in Spanish as you put the numerals 1 to 10 in the upper-left corner of the appropriate square for this month. Stop at 10.

To complete your calendar, you need to become familiar with the numbers from 11 to 31. Here they are:

Los números de 11 a 31

		20	**veinte**	30	**treinta**
11	**once**	21	**veintiuno**	31	**treinta y uno**
12	**doce**	22	**veintidós**		
13	**trece**	23	**veintitrés**		
14	**catorce**	24	**veinticuatro**		
15	**quince**	25	**veinticinco**		
16	**dieciséis**	26	**veintiséis**		
17	**diecisiete**	27	**veintisiete**		
18	**dieciocho**	28	**veintiocho**		
19	**diecinueve**	29	**veintinueve**		

Together with your teacher and classmates, say the **números**. Then write the **números** you need into your calendar, saying them softly to yourself. Now your calendar is complete, and you're ready to plan important dates for your homestay.

LA FECHA (THE DATE)

In addition to the date (**la fecha**) on a calendar, you will see dates in newspapers, magazines, and TV listings, as well as on tickets and advertisements for events. Examine the **fechas** below, which appear on items you're likely to see in your homestay country.

2 de enero de 1993

13/8/94

16 de junio de 1994

Domingo, el 14 de septiembre de 1995

21/5/93

24 de octubre de 1994

What do you notice about the way dates are shown in Spanish-speaking countries? That's exactly right! The month and day are reversed from the way we show them in the United States. Here's a little practice to sharpen your eye for the way dates are written in Spanish-speaking countries.

Match the Spanish and English dates below. Put the letter of the Spanish date in the blank next to the corresponding date in English. The first one is done for you.

A. el 15 de febrero   1. _____ July 25th

B. el 25 de diciembre   2. _____ April 1st

C. el 12 de marzo   3. _____ December 25th

D. el 1° de mayo   4. _____ March 12th

E. el 25 de julio   5. _____ September 15th

F. el 12 de octubre   6. _____ October 12th

G. el 1° de abril   7. _____ May 1st

H. el 15 de septiembre   8. __A__ February 15th

Nota When Spanish speakers talk of the first day of each month, they use the words **el primero** or **el primer día**. For example:

el primero de enero   *the first of January*
el primer día de enero   *the first day of January*

Study the dates in the activity above. How do Spanish speakers write **primero** as a numeral?

_____

G. LA FECHA ESCRITA EN NÚMEROS (THE DATE IN NUMERALS)

In Activity F you learned about using words to write dates in Spanish. Sometimes you will see a date written entirely in numerals (**en números**). When numerals are used to write a date in Spanish-speaking countries, they are written in the same order as dates using words: day/month. So May 3 is written in Spanish as 3/5 (the third day of the fifth month). This same date could be written as **el tres de mayo**. Remember these differences when you make plans with your Spanish-speaking friends. You don't want to miss an important event, do you?

Look at the dates below. They are written the way you will see them in your homestay country.

10/2	el 10 de febrero
6/4	el 6 de abril
12/9	el 12 de septiembre

Have you figured out the pattern?

Write your birthday in numerals as you would write it in a Spanish-speaking country._____

Then write out your birthday using words._____

Practicing dates will help you prepare for your homestay experience. Why not practice by planning when you'll make payments for your homestay? Payments are due every two months from the date of the first payment. Look at the example below. The first column shows the date when the first payment of money for the trip is due. Calculate the date of your next payment. Write this date in both numerals and words.

Example: el 13 de mayo (+ 2 meses = el 13 de julio)   *13/7   el trece de julio*

1. el 10 de febrero   _____   _____

2. el 1º de marzo   _____   _____

3. el 7 de julio   _____   _____

4. el 30 de octubre   _____   _____

5. el 29 de agosto   _____   _____

6. el 25 de abril   _____   _____

7. el 13 de junio   _____   _____

When you finish, check your answers with the rest of the class. Your teacher will help you.

H. DOS PASAPORTES
(TWO PASSPORTS)

You'll need to get a passport (**un pasaporte**) to travel to most other countries. Review the information in Kristina Sullivan's **pasaporte**.

Now look at the Mexican **pasaporte** belonging to Enrique Carmona. Compare the two **pasaportes**. Do you see any of the same information?

Compare the information presented in Kristina's and Enrique's **pasaportes**. Then, answer the questions below.

1. **Apellido**   ¿de Kristina? _____

                           ¿de Enrique? _____

2. **Fecha de nacimiento** ¿de Kristina? _____

                           ¿de Enrique? _____

3. **Teléfono**   ¿de Kristina? _____

                           ¿de Enrique? _____

4. **Color de los ojos**   ¿de Kristina? _____

                           ¿de Enrique? _____

5. **Dirección**   ¿de Kristina? _____

                           ¿de Enrique? _____

Circle the best response for these passport questions.

1. ¿Fecha de nacimiento?

   a. Carmona   b. 5-521-79-53   c. México, D.F.   d. 27/3/83

2. ¿Apellido?

   a. Sullivan   b. Kristina   c. 313-296-4157   d. 5-521-79-53

3. ¿Teléfono?

   a. Sullivan   b. Kristina   c. 313-296-4157   d. 7/9/83

4. ¿Color del pelo?

   a. Carmona   b. negro   c. 7/9/83   d. Enrique

5. ¿Dirección?

   a. 5-521-79-53   b. Carmona   c. 27 Independencia   d. 27/3/83

I. SOLICITUD PARA MI PASAPORTE
(APPLICATION FOR MY PASSPORT)

Part 1. Now it's time to apply for your passport. Your teacher will give you a copy of the application form. Look at Kristina's and Enrique's **pasaportes** if you need help.

Part 2. When you land at the airport in your homestay country, your first stop will be to have your passport checked. To help you get ready, your teacher will give you the forms to make a **pasaporte** for classroom practice. After you make it, practice presenting it to the immigration officer. Your teacher will show you what to do.

MI DIARIO (MY JOURNAL)

Select five to ten new Spanish words from Element 3 that you need to remember. Write them under **Mis palabras**. Don't forget to record new information in your journal under **Información nueva**.

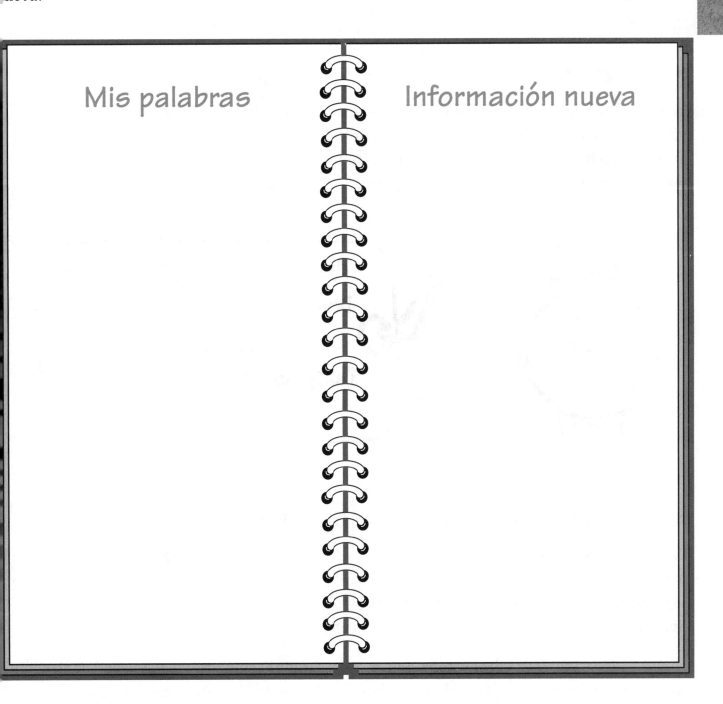

Mis palabras

Información nueva

TRAVEL DETAILS

PERSPECTIVA

Your trip is beginning to take shape. With your **pasaporte** in hand and your knowledge about your host country, you'll soon be ready for your trip. In this Element, you prepare information about yourself that will be given to your host family before your visit. You also learn how to tell time and how to complete a luggage tag. **¿Listos? ¡Vámonos!**

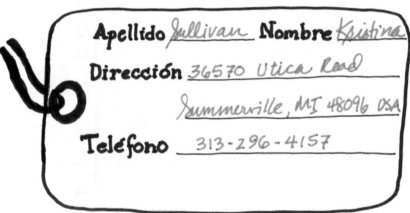

A. FORMULARIO DE DATOS PERSONALES

Preparations for your homestay are progressing very well! You are learning about the country and how to say some essential words and phrases in Spanish. Remember—if you need to ask how to say something in Spanish, ask **¿Cómo se dice _____ en español?** (*How do you say _____ in Spanish?*) It will be a useful question when you are with your host family.

Now it's time to complete the Personal Information Form (**Formulario de datos personales**). This is your way of introducing yourself to your host family, and helping them get to know you. Opposite is a copy of the form that Kristina Sullivan completed last year. It has two parts. Look at the first part. Circle the words that are new to you. Can you guess what they mean? Do you recognize any words from the passport activity in Element 3? If you need help with new words, ask your teacher.

DATOS PERSONALES

Apellido _Sullivan_

Nombre _Kristina_

Edad _12 años_

Dirección _36570 Utica Road_

Summerville, Michigan 48096

Teléfono _313-296-4157_

Escuela _Summerville Middle School_

Maestro(a) de español _Señora Strutzel_

Padres _Dale y Susan Sullivan_

Yo tengo __2__ hermano(s) __1__ hermana(s)

Yo tengo

☑ perro   ☐ gato   ☑ pez

☐ caballo   ☐ pájaro

In the second part, Kristina noted her favorite activities (**actividades favoritos**) and favorite sports (**deportes favoritos**) so that her host family would know about her favorite pastimes. To do this, Kristina used two expressions that you will also need to use: **Me gusta** (*I like*) and **No me gusta** (*I don't like*). Review Kristina's favorite pastimes. The pictures next to the words will help you understand their meanings.

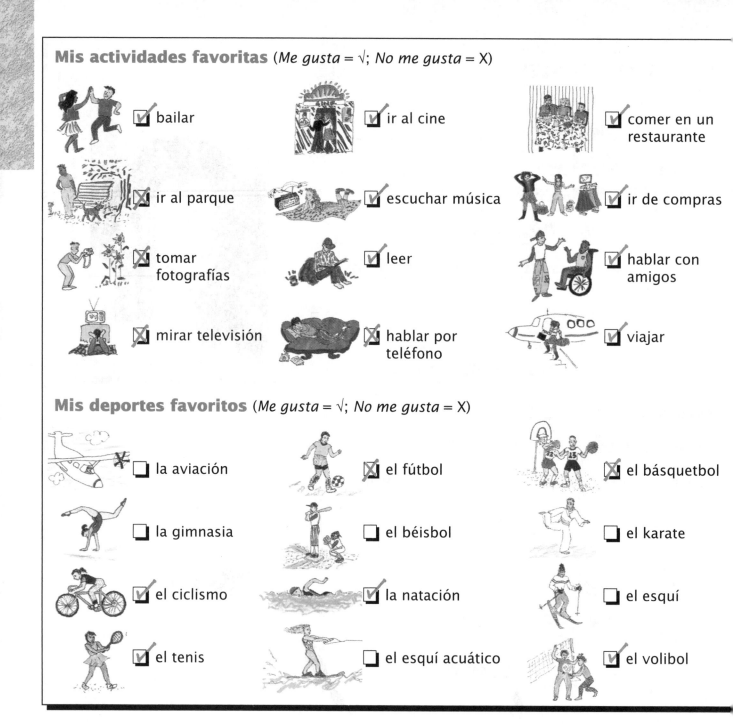

Mis actividades favoritas (*Me gusta* = √; *No me gusta* = X)

- ☑ bailar
- ☑ ir al cine
- ☑ comer en un restaurante
- ☒ ir al parque
- ☑ escuchar música
- ☑ ir de compras
- ☒ tomar fotografías
- ☑ leer
- ☑ hablar con amigos
- ☒ mirar televisión
- ☒ hablar por teléfono
- ☑ viajar

Mis deportes favoritos (*Me gusta* = √; *No me gusta* = X)

- ☐ la aviación
- ☒ el fútbol
- ☒ el básquetbol
- ☐ la gimnasia
- ☐ el béisbol
- ☐ el karate
- ☑ el ciclismo
- ☑ la natación
- ☐ el esquí
- ☑ el tenis
- ☐ el esquí acuático
- ☑ el volibol

B. LLENAR EL FORMULARIO

Kristina Sullivan's **Formulario de datos personales** gave the host family information about her before she arrived. Now you need to fill out a form for your own homestay. Remember that the phrases **Me gusta** and **No me gusta** mean *I like* and *I don't like.* You will use them often as you travel. For now, look at the pictures and indicate which activities or sports you like or don't like. The pictures give clues to the meaning of the words and phrases. Please start with the **Datos personales**. ¿Listos? ¡Vámonos!

DATOS PERSONALES

Apellido _____ Nombre _____ Edad _____

Dirección _____ Teléfono _____

Escuela _____ Maestro(a) de español _____

Padres _____ Yo tengo _____ hermano(s) _____ hermana(s)

Yo tengo ☐ perro ☐ gato ☐ caballo ☐ pájaro ☐ pez

Mis actividades favoritas (*Me gusta* = √; *No me gusta* = X)

☐ bailar ☐ ir al cine ☐ comer en un restaurante

☐ ir al parque ☐ escuchar música ☐ ir de compras

☐ tomar fotografías ☐ leer ☐ hablar con amigos

☐ mirar televisión ☐ hablar por teléfono ☐ viajar

Mis deportes favoritos (*Me gusta* = √; *No me gusta* = X)

☐ la aviación ☐ el fútbol ☐ el básquetbol

☐ la gimnasia ☐ el béisbol ☐ el karate

☐ el ciclismo ☐ la natación ☐ el esquí

☐ el tenis ☐ el esquí acuático ☐ el volibol

C. ORGANIZACIÓN PARA EL VIAJE

In Element 3, you learned **los días de la semana**. Here is a page from Kristina's planning calendar from last year. Review the **días** and the things she did. As you review, think about your own trip and how you will organize your own list of travel preparations.

JUNIO

lunes 12	*Prepare album of family and friends*
martes 13	*Purchase traveler's checks*
miércoles 14	*Buy travel journal*
jueves 15	*Buy a gift for host family*
viernes 16	*Record addresses of family and friends*
sábado 17	*Pack suitcase*
domingo 18	*Say good-bye to friends*

fter reviewing Kristina's calendar, read the statements below. Pay careful attention to the **días** to etermine if each statement is true (**verdadero**) or false (**falso**). Check (√) the correct answer.

	Verdadero	Falso
Kristina packed her suitcase on Saturday.	_____	_____
She bought a gift for her host family on Monday.	_____	_____
Kristina purchased traveler's checks on Thursday.	_____	_____
She said good-bye to friends on Sunday.	_____	_____
She bought her travel journal on Wednesday.	_____	_____
Kristina traveled in July.	_____	_____

D. ORGANIZACIÓN DE LA SEMANA

ook at the post-it notes below. Each drawing should jog your memory about something you need do before you leave. Decide on which day of the week (**día de la semana**) you have time for ach task. Write the Spanish word for that day next to **día** on each note. You also have two blank otes for additional tasks. If you wish to use these extra notes, put a picture and a related word on ach. Use your time wisely. Plan to complete at least one task per day, but don't list them all for he same day.

E. COMPARAR ENTRE AMIGOS

You now have your schedule of things to do for the week. Get together with another student who will also be going on a homestay to compare schedules. Coordinating your efforts can save time and energy. Partner A reads the activity from the grid below. Partner B responds by telling the **día** that he or she will complete the task. Check the **día** you hear for each task. Switch roles.

ACTIVIDAD	lunes	martes	miércoles	jueves	viernes	sábado	domingo
buy travel journal							
pack suitcase							
prepare family photo album							
say good-bye to friends							
record family/friends addresses							
buy traveler's checks							
buy gift for host family							

When you have finished, look at the two grids. Did both of you plan things for the same **día**? If no, check (√) **no** ____. If yes, check (√) **sí** ____. Decide how you will share the responsibility for getting these things done.

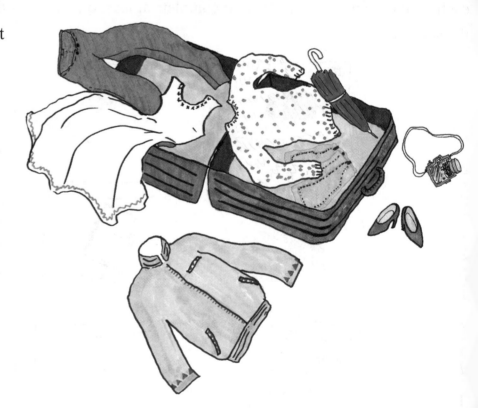

E. ¿QUÉ HORA ES?

Your trip will involve many scheduled activities. Understanding how time is expressed in Spanish will be very important. You already know the numbers from 1 to 31. Quietly say the numbers from 1 to 12 as a review. When you want to say *It's 2:00 o'clock* in Spanish, you say **Son las dos**. Look at the clocks below and say the times shown on each clock. Remember to begin with **Son las**. Watch out for *one o'clock*! It's a little different.

Son las doce can refer to noon or midnight. You'll want to be able to express the difference.

¿**Cómo se dice** *It's noon* **en español?**   **Se dice** *Es mediodía.*

¿**Cómo se dice** *It's midnight* **en español?**   **Se dice** *Es medianoche.*

A.

B.

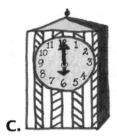
C.

D.

E.

F.

G.

H.

Using your skill with numbers, match the times on the clocks above with the words below. Put the letter of the clock in the blank that indicates the time shown on the clock.

1. _____ Son las seis.

2. _____ Son las once.

3. _____ Son las cinco.

4. _____ Es la una.

5. _____ Son las dos.

6. _____ Son las diez.

7. _____ Es medianoche

8. _____ Es mediodía.

9. _____ _____ Son las doce.

Easy, isn't it? **Fácil, ¿verdad?**

How do you say *It's 1:00*?_____

Why is it different from the other hours?_____

G. UN RELOJ

Now let's make a clock (**un reloj**). To do this project you will need:

- a small paper plate
- a piece of cardboard to make the hands of the clock
- a brad or fastener
- crayons or markers to write numbers
- scissors

Instructions:

1. Cut out two clock hands, one somewhat longer than the other.
2. Punch holes in the center of the plate and near the end of each hand.
3. Attach the two hands to the plate with the fastener.
4. Write the numbers on the face of the clock.
5. Decorate the face of the clock.

You are now ready for some clock activities. First, your teacher will say a time of day in Spanish. Set your clock by moving the hands to show the time. Hold your clock up as soon as you have set it. Next, work with a partner. Each of you should make a list of five different "on-the-hour" times. Now, say the times to your partner and your partner will set his or her clock to show the correct time. Switch roles. You can keep a tally of the number of correct responses. Keep the clock because you will use it again as you study time in more detail.

1. ¿A QUÉ HORA?

You have now learned how to tell time. For example, *It's 5:00* = **Son las cinco**. To say at what time something happens, you just change the first word: *at 5:00* = **a las cinco**. If you want to ask *at what time*, ask: **¿A que hora...?**

Look at this example:

It's 5:00. Let's go!	**Son las cinco. ¡Vámonos!**
I like to watch TV at 5:00.	**Me gusta mirar la televisión a las cinco.**

A las doce can mean either *at noon* or *at midnight*. To specify which one you mean, you can say either **al mediodía** or **a la medianoche**.

In this exercise you will use the phrase that tells at what time something happens. Here is a list of some activities that are scheduled during your homestay. Review the schedule sheet, then listen as the starting time for each activity is announced by your teacher. Place a check mark (√) in the box of the announced time.

ACTIVIDAD	1:00	2:00	3:00	4:00	5:00	6:00	7:00	8:00	9:00	10:00	11:00	12:00
ir de compras												
ir a un concierto												
ir a un museo												
ir a un partido de fútbol												
comer												
ir a la escuela												
jugar al tenis												
hablar por teléfono												
ir al cine												

I. ETIQUETA DE EQUIPAJE

The travel agency will send you a blank luggage tag (**etiqueta de equipaje**) for your suitcase. In your homestay country you will be asked to fill out a different tag for your return trip. It will look like the one below. Read the Spanish instructions carefully. Complete the **etiqueta de equipaje** with your **datos personales**.

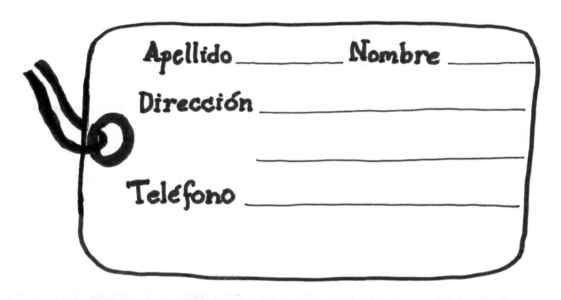

Apellido _____ Nombre _____

Dirección _____

_____

Teléfono _____

Viaje en un tren de película.

Viaje con coche, en tren.

MI DIARIO

Record new information in your **diario**. Include facts about yourself that you want your host family to know. Remember to use **Me gusta** and **No me gusta** to describe your favorite **actividades** and **deportes**. This information will let them know more about you. Write this information under **información nueva**. Select five to ten new Spanish words from Element 4 that you need to remember. Write these words under **Mis palabras**.

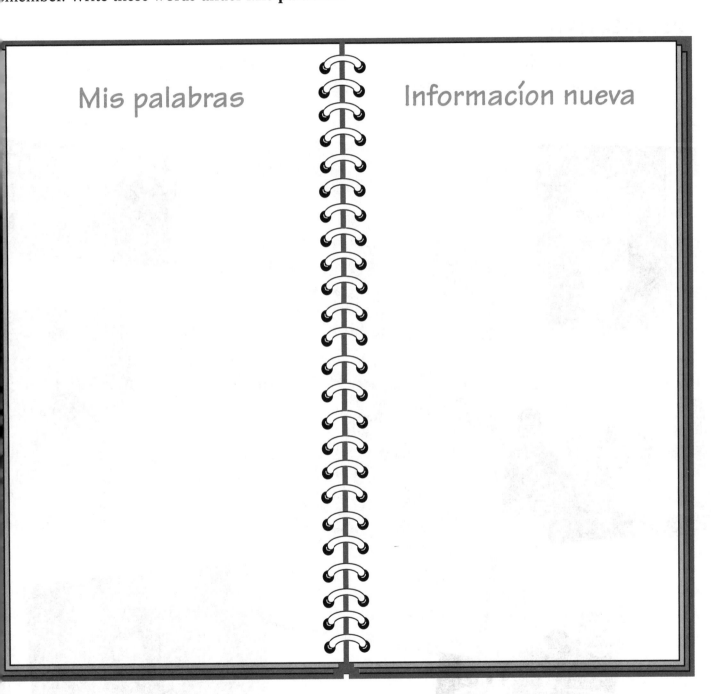

Mis palabras

Información nueva

5

EXCHANGING LETTERS
WITH YOUR HOST FAMILY

PERSPECTIVA

Your passport has arrived! It's time to select your host family and begin writing to them.
Exchanging letters and pictures will help you get acquainted.

el 15 de abril

¡Hola!
Quiero presentarme. Me llamo Alejandro. Gracias
por tu carta y las fotos. Me gustaron mucho.
Soy estudiante en el séptimo grado. Mi escuela
se llama Academia Central. Tengo 12 años.
Me gusta nadar, jugar al fútbol y jugar al
tenis. También estudio inglés en la escuela.
Tenemos mucho en común.

Aquí está una foto de mi familia. Hay cuatro
personas en mi familia. Mi hermana se llama
Gloria. No tengo hermanos. Tengo dos amigos
especiales. Se llaman Eduardo y Jaime. Me
gustan los animales. Tengo un perro y un pájaro.
Pero no tengo un gato.

Estoy esperando tu visita. Hay mucho que hacer
aquí. No te olvides una raqueta de tenis. Hay
un campo de tenis cerca de la casa. Ya tienes
mi dirección y mi número de teléfono.

Hasta junio,

Alejandro

LOS NÚMEROS DE 10 A 1.000

e organization in charge of the homestay program will send you a list of host families. You will
ect your homestay family from this list. Won't it be exciting to learn about them? The list will
o give each family's **dirección** and **número de teléfono**. These will be very important for you to
member, because they will be your **dirección** and **número de teléfono** for the duration of your
mestay! Your friends and family here in the United States will need this information, too. They
y want to call or write to you while you're away. It's also a good idea for them to have these
mbers in case of an emergency.

understand and give your homestay **dirección** and **número de teléfono** in Spanish, you need
know **los números** from 10 to 1,000.

ok at the numbers below. Which ones do you already know? Count quietly to yourself as your
cher counts aloud. Count by tens from 10 to 100, starting with **diez**. Then, starting with **cien**,
ntinue counting by hundreds from 100 to 1,000.

10	**diez**	100	**cien**
20	**veinte**	200	**doscientos**
30	**treinta**	300	**trescientos**
40	**cuarenta**	400	**cuatrocientos**
50	**cincuenta**	500	**quinientos**
60	**sesenta**	600	**seiscientos**
70	**setenta**	700	**setecientos**
80	**ochenta**	800	**ochocientos**
90	**noventa**	900	**novecientos**
100	**cien**	1.000	**mil**

Look at the way Spanish speakers write the numeral for one thousand. In Spanish,
one thousand is sometimes written with a period (1.000) and sometimes with a
space (1 000). Both forms are understood in Spanish-speaking countries.

Spanish speakers use **ciento** when the number is more than 100.
For example: **120 = ciento veinte**.

actice counting by tens or hundreds starting from 10, 12, or 15. Your teacher will tell you
nat to do.

ow that you know these higher numbers, you're ready to learn your new **dirección** and **número**
e **teléfono**.

B. DIRECCIÓN Y NÚMERO DE TELÉFONO DE MI FAMILIA

You're ready to make your homestay selection. Here is the list of host families. They live in severa different Spanish-speaking countries. In Element 1, there are maps to help you locate these countries. Now, select a host family and a country for your homestay. Choose your family from the list. Put a check mark (√) next to your choice.

❏ **Sr. y Sra. Danilo Zapatero**
J. J. Pasos 470
Pueblo Libre-Lima 21
Perú
(51) 14-231-4030

❏ **Sr. y Sra. Luís de la Cruz**
Avenida de la Reforma 96
México, D.F.
México
(52) 5-545-6540

❏ **Sr. y Sra. Javier Gonzalez**
Avenida Benito Juárez 55
Maracaibo
Venezuela
(58) 61-123-2240

❏ **Sr. y Sra. Héctor Bueno**
Calle Industrial 29
Quito
Ecuador
(593) 2-483-1288

❏ **Sr. y Sra. José-Luís Santa María**
Calle Bolívar 3
La Paz
Bolivia
(591) 2-51-1570

❏ **Sr. y Sra. Guillermo Blandón**
Avenida Cervantes 96
Madrid
España
(34) 1-174-6892

❏ **Sr. y Sra. Roberto Rodriguez**
Avenida Mayor 56
Guatemala City
Guatemala
(502) 2-25-4103

❏ **Sr. y Sra. Armando Ramírez**
Avenida Martín Fierro 88
Buenos Aires
Argentina
(54) 1-437-6852

❏ **Sr. y Sra. Orlando Villegas**
Calle el Greco 16
Toledo
España
(34) 25-614-0520

❏ **Sr. y Sra. Rubén Torres**
Calle Kukulkán 95
Cancun
México
(52) 98-338-2941

❏ **Sr. y Sra. Fernando Sánchez**
Avenida Ponce de León 27
San Juan
Puerto Rico
(809) 672-4330

❏ **Sr. y Sra. Miguel Bazán**
Avenida de la Independencia 67
Bogotá
Colombia
(57) 1-473-5110

Nota When you telephone outside of the United States, U.S. territories, or Canada, you need to know the country code. These codes may have two or three digits. If you are calling another country, you need to dial the country code before the home number of the person you are calling.

. What is the **apellido** of the homestay family you have chosen? _____

. What is their country code? _____

. When you are in your homestay city, what number would you dial to call your homestay

family if you needed to? _____

CARTA Y SOBRE

ach student who participates in a homestay writes a letter (**una carta**) to the host family before
he homestay begins. You've chosen your host family and you have their **dirección**. Address an
nvelope (**un sobre**) to them. Put your return address in the upper-left corner. Use the envelope
elow to practice.

_____
_____
_____
_____

                                    _____
                                      _____
                                      _____
                                      _____

D. LA CARTA DE KRISTINA

In Element 4, you completed a Personal Information Form to give your host family some information about yourself. A letter (**una carta**) is an additional and more personal part of your introduction. Below is the letter Kristina Sullivan wrote to the Carmonas last year. Read it three times. Read first for general meaning. (You don't have to know every word to understand the main idea. Remember to look for cognates.) The second time you read the letter, if you need more help, refer to the English meanings of the new words (**palabras nuevas**) written in the side column. Finally, read **la carta** again for further detail and practice.

10 de abril,

Estimados Señor y Señora Carmona,

Quiero presentarme. Me llamo Kristina Sullivan. Soy estudiante en Summerville Middle School. Tengo 12 años. Me gusta nadar, jugar al tenis y leer cómicos. Estudio español.

Aquí está una foto de mi familia. Hay seis personas en mi familia: mi papá, mi mamá, mis dos hermanos, mi hermana y yo. También hay un perro y un pez.

Llego al aeropuerto el 23 de junio a las diez de la noche. El número del vuelo es Air Alpha 672. Estoy entusiasmada de poder estar en su casa. Muchas gracias.

Sinceramente,

Kristina

PALABRAS NUEVAS

Quiero presentarme I wa[nt] to introduce myself
soy I am
estudiante student
nadar to swim
jugar al tenis to play tenn[is]
estudio I study

una foto a photo
hay there is/there are

hermanos brothers
hermana sister

llego I arrive/I am arriving
al aeropuerto at the airpo[rt]
de la noche at night
del vuelo of the flight
estoy entusiasmada I'm excited
poder estar to be able to b[e]
casa home/house

E. TU CARTA

You've read Kristina's letter from last year. Below is an outline to help you write your own letter. Use it to complete your first draft. Then, with a partner, read your draft and discuss possible changes. Rewrite a final copy of your letter. You may write this final copy on a nice sheet of stationery or compose it on a computer. Keep your final copy in a safe place. You may decide to include it in your **diario**.

el _____ de _____
    (date)   *(month)*

Estimados Señor y Señora _____ ,

Quiero presentarme. _____ . _____ estudiante en
                           (My name is . . .)   *(I am)*

_____ . Tengo _____ años. _____ _____
    (your school name)   *(your age)*   *(I like)*   *(activity)*

y _____ . Estudio _____ .
   (sport)   *(Spanish)*

Aquí está una _____ de mi _____ . _____ _____ personas
           (photo)   *(family)*   *(There are)*   *(number)*

en mi familia: _____ .
                   (list of members of your family)

También hay _____ y _____ .
           (list of your pets—number and type)

Llego al _____ el _____ a la una de la tarde (*in the*
      (airport)   *(June 23)*

afternoon). El número del vuelo es Beta Air 793. _____ de poder
                                            (I am excited)

estar en su casa.

Sinceramente,

_____
           (your signature)

F. LA RESPUESTA

This is truly exciting! Your host family received your letter and their son, Alejandro, answered it. Read the response (**la respuesta**) carefully three times. Read first for general meaning. Remember to look for cognates. The second time, if you need more help, refer to the English meanings of the **palabras nuevas** written in the side column. Then, read it again for further detail and practice.

el 15 de abril

Hola!
Quiero presentarme. Me llamo Alejandro. Gracias por tu carta y las fotos. Me gustaron mucho. Soy estudiante en el séptimo grado. Mi escuela se llama Academia Central. Tengo 12 años. Me gusta nadar, jugar al fútbol y jugar al tenis. También estudio inglés en la escuela. Tenemos mucho en común.

Aquí está una foto de mi familia. Hay cuatro personas en mi familia. Mi hermana se llama Gloria. No tengo hermanos. Tengo dos amigos especiales. Se llaman Eduardo y Jaime. Me gustan los animales. Tengo un perro y un pájaro. Pero no tengo un gato.

Estoy esperando tu visita. Hay mucho que hacer aquí. No te olvides una raqueta de tenis. Hay un campo de tenis cerca de la casa. Ya tienes mi dirección y mi número de teléfono.

Hasta junio,

Alejandro

PALABRAS NUEVAS
Hola Hi
Me gustaron mucho I liked them a lot
el séptimo grado the 7th grade
también too
jugar al fútbol to play soccer
estudio inglés I study English
en la escuela in school
en común in common

Estoy esperando I'm waiting for
tu visita your visit
mucho que hacer a lot to do
No te olvides don't forget
tu raqueta de tenis your tennis raquet
un campo de tenis tennis court
cerca de la casa near the house
Ya tienes you already have
Hasta until

G. FOTOS DE LA FAMILIA

Pictures as well as letters get you better acquainted with your homestay family. After reading Alejandro's **carta**, locate the pictures of the family (**fotos de la familia**), friends, and pets on page 60. Look at their pictures below. Write their names below the pictures. This will help you recognize them when you arrive.

La familia de Alejandro

Los amigos de Alejandro

H. PRIMERA IMPRESIÓN

Have you heard the saying, "One picture is worth a thousand words?" Do you think it's true? Pictures often give us our first impression (**primera impresión**) of people. Look at **las fotos de la familia de Alejandro**. What are your first impressions? Now look below at some Spanish words that can be used to describe someone's personality. Choose one of these words to describe each important person in Alejandro's life. Write that word by the appropriate picture on page 57. Be careful! There's also another saying that "looks can be deceiving." After meeting them, you may change your **primera impresión**. Some of the words have two forms. If you need help selecting the correct form of the word, go back to Element 2 or ask your teacher.

extrovertido(a)	egoísta	valiente	generoso(a)
tímido(a)	trabajador(a)	obediente	envidioso(a)
sentimental	cariñoso(a)	ambicioso(a)	hablador(a)
independiente	arrogante	espontáneo(a)	simpático(a)
perezoso(a)	activo(a)	indeciso(a)	quieto(a)

IMPRESIONES

You've learned some Spanish words to describe personality characteristics, and you've given your first impressions of Alejandro's family. Now think about yourself. Look at the list of characteristics and qualities in Activity H. Choose your two strongest positive characteristics and write them in the blank in the sentence beginning with **Soy** (*I am*).

Soy _____ y _____ .

Next, think of someone you know and admire. Write his or her name in the first blank of the following sentence. Complete the sentence by listing five characteristics you see in this person.

_____ es (*is*) _____ , _____ ,

_____ , _____ y _____ .

Share the description above with a partner. Talk more about why you admire the person you chose.

J. UN REGALO

When staying in someone's home in a Spanish-speaking country, it is customary to bring a gift (**un regalo**). When you participate in a homestay experience, it is important to do things that are culturally appropriate and show your good manners. **Un regalo** is your way of saying thank you to your host family for opening their home to you and letting you participate in their lives. This **regalo** is also a way of sharing a part of your culture. It does not have to be big and expensive, but it should be selected with thoughtfulness and care. Your host family might particularly enjoy something you have made or a special souvenir of the city, state, or region where you live, such as local handicrafts or products, or a book of pictures about your area.

To help you decide on a gift, look below at the idea webs. Working with two or three of your classmates, brainstorm ideas for these webs. Fill in the cells with suggestions from your group. If you wish, add additional cells. Then, when all of the group ideas have been shared, try to agree on the most appropriate gift.

REGALOS

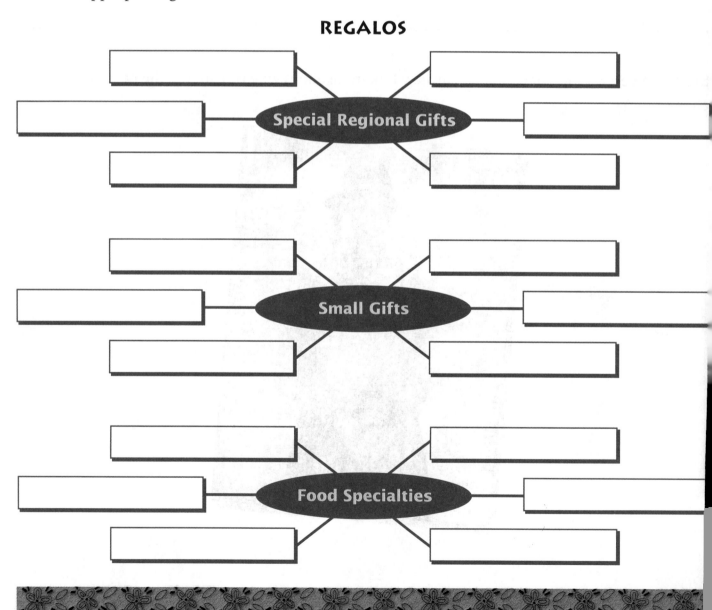

C. MI DIARIO

Select five to ten new Spanish words from this Element that you need to remember. Write them under **Mis palabras**. Under **Regalo** include a drawing or a picture of the gift you have chosen to give your host family. Also, record new information in your journal under **Información nueva**. You may want to include the **carta** you wrote to your host family or you may want to describe your first impression of someone you met recently.

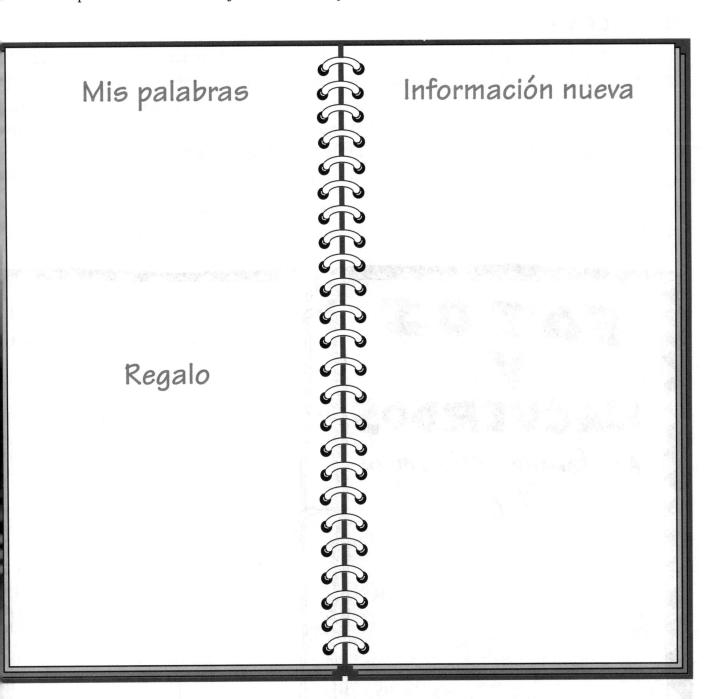

Mis palabras

Información nueva

Regalo

PREPARING A PHOTO ALBUM

PERSPECTIVA

In Elements 1 through 5 you have prepared for your homestay experience. You've learned about your homestay country, chosen a host family, packed your clothes, applied for a **pasaporte**, written to your host family and received a letter from them. You're almost ready to go! In Element 6 you are going to construct a photo album that organizes **fotos** and special memories (**recuerdos**) about your life in the United States to show your host family and new friends.

Your album is also a review of the Spanish you have learned in Elements 1 through 5. Your teacher may give you an Organization and Assessment Grid to help assess your project. As you organize your album (**tu álbum**), keep the criteria on the grid in mind. Have fun!

TU VIDA

Your homestay family will want to see what your life (**tu vida**) is like in the United States. To show them, you will construct a photo album to take with you on your homestay. It is a reflection of you, your family, your friends, your neighborhood, and your favorite activities and sports. Remember that your host family speaks Spanish, so you'll need to use as much Spanish as possible in your album. Begin by designing a cover page for your album. As you prepare your album, think about what is important in your daily life.

B. YO

Your host family will want to get to know you when you arrive. Your photo album is an interesting way to share your life with them. Start the album by showing yourself and all the things you like to do. **Yo** means *I*. Place two different pictures or drawings of yourself in each space labeled **Yo.** Writ some information about yourself below each picture. To get you started, some suggested sentences are started below. Don't limit yourself to the starter sentences, however. Be creative. There may be many things you'd like to share with the host family through **fotos** or **dibujos**. Be sure to label each photo and drawing in Spanish. If you need help, use a dictionary, or ask your classmates or teache

YO

Me llamo _____.

Mi cumpleaños es _____.

Tengo _____ años.

_____

_____

YO

Me gustan_____

_____.

Soy_____

_____

_____.

C. MI FAMILIA

our host family and new friends will also be very interested in your family (**tu familia**). Place
hotos or drawings of your family in the spaces labeled **Mi familia**. Write some information about
hem below the pictures. Use the sentence starters, if you want, but don't limit yourself to them.
ou may want to include additional information about your family. Maybe you can tell what they
re like. If you need help, use a dictionary, or ask your classmates or teacher.

MI FAMILIA

En mi familia hay _____ personas.

Mi papá se llama _____.

Tiene _____ años.

Mi mamá se llama _____.

Tiene _____ años.

_____

_____

MI FAMILIA

Mis hermanos y mis hermanas se

llaman _____

_____.

Tienen _____ años.

_____

_____

D. MI CASA Y MI VECINDAD

Your home (**tu casa**) and your neighborhood (**tu vecindad**) will be interesting to your homestay family. They'll want to know how they differ from **casas** or **apartamentos** in their country. Show pictures of your home and neighborhood, so that the homestay family will have a clear idea of what they are like. Describe your home and neighborhood from the pictures.

MI CASA

Mi dirección es _____

_____

_____

_____.

Mi número de teléfono es_____

_____

_____.

MI VECINDAD

Mi vecindad se llama _____.

Está en_____.
                    (city, state)

En mi vecindad hay _____
                    (points of interest)

_____

_____

_____

_____.

MIS AMIGOS

You'll make new friends while you're on your homestay. They will want to know about your friends (**tus amigos**) in your hometown. Include **fotos** or **dibujos** and descriptions of your friends in your album. Use the words you learned earlier to describe their characteristics and personalities. Place the pictures in the spaces labeled **Mis amigos.**

MIS AMIGOS/AMIGAS

Mis amigos/amigas se llaman _____

_____.

Tienen _____ años.

_____

_____

_____

MIS AMIGOS/AMIGAS

Les gustan (*They like*) _____

_____.

Son _____
                    (description)

_____

_____

_____.

F. MI ESCUELA

You'll attend school in your homestay country, too. While you're there, the new teachers and students will be curious about the school you attend in your hometown. Include a **foto** or **dibujo** of your school in the space labeled **Mi escuela**. Also put a picture of your class in the space labeled **Mi clase**. Then write information about your school and class that your new friends will find interesting.

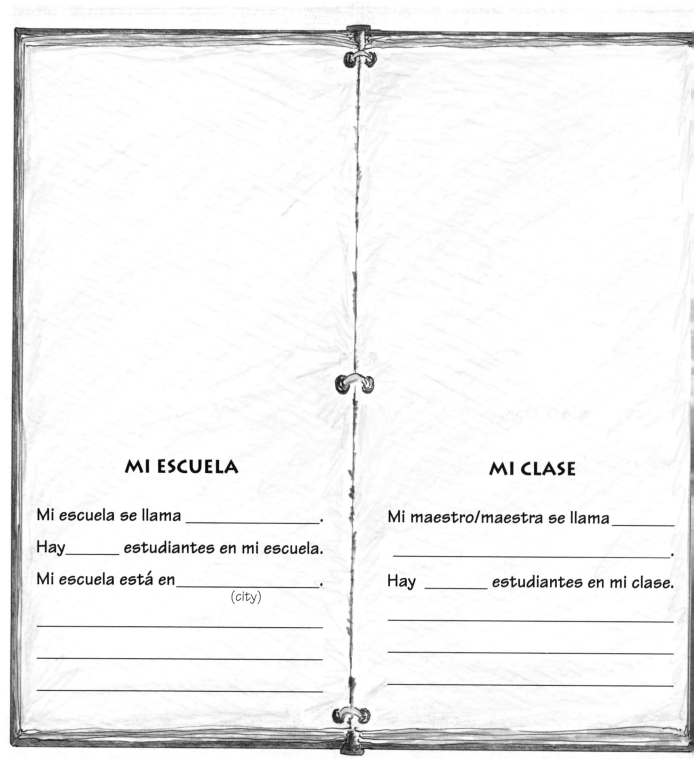

MI ESCUELA

Mi escuela se llama _____.

Hay_____ estudiantes en mi escuela.

Mi escuela está en_____.
                                 (city)

_____

_____

_____

MI CLASE

Mi maestro/maestra se llama_____

_____.

Hay _____ estudiantes en mi clase.

_____

_____

_____

G. MIS ACTIVIDADES FAVORITAS

Every student has favorite activities. In your **formulario de datos personales** and your **carta**, you talked about your **actividades favoritas**. In your album, put photos and drawings that show how you spend your free time. Show at least one on each page of your album.

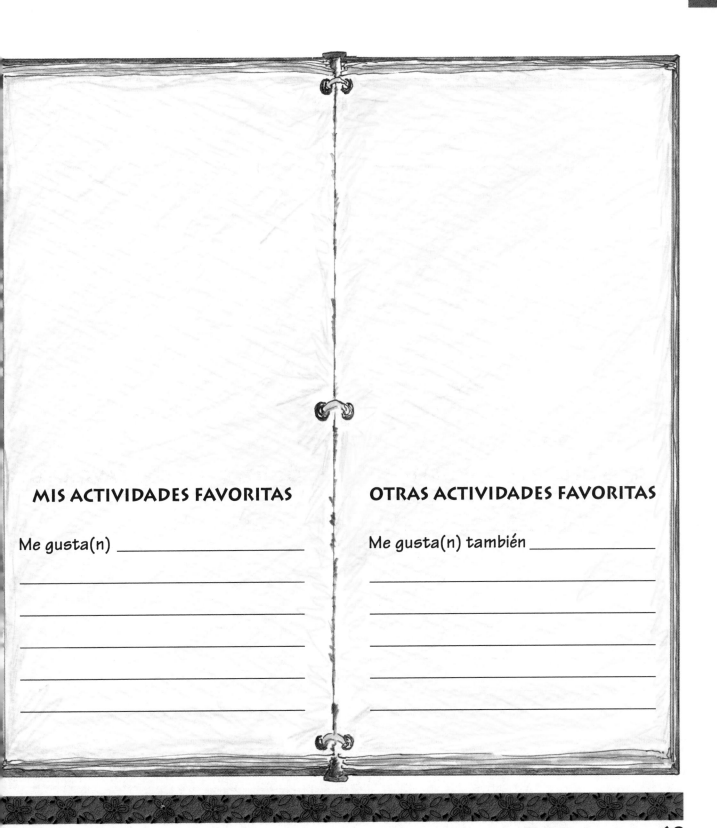

MIS ACTIVIDADES FAVORITAS

Me gusta(n) _____

_____

_____

_____

_____

OTRAS ACTIVIDADES FAVORITAS

Me gusta(n) también _____

_____

_____

_____

_____

H. MIS DEPORTES FAVORITOS

You may also want to tell your host family about your favorite sports; those you play and those you watch. In your album, put photos and drawings that show you playing your **deportes favoritos** or that show the kinds of **deportes** you like to watch. Show at least one on each page of your album.

MIS DEPORTES FAVORITOS

Me gusta(n) _____

_____

_____

_____

_____

OTROS DEPORTES FAVORITOS

Me gusta(n) también _____

_____

_____

_____

_____

MI ANIMAL FAVORITO Y OTRAS COSAS IMPORTANTES

Pets (**los animales favoritos**) are an important part of many students' lives. If you have **un animal favorito**, remember to include a picture of it in your album. If you don't have a pet, show what kind of pet you might like to have. Then write some information about your pet below the picture. Think about some other important things (**otras cosas importantes**) that you might want to share with your homestay family and friends. Include drawings or photos if you want to, and write information about these things.

MI ANIMAL FAVORITO

Tengo _____

_____ .

Se llama _____

_____ .

_____

_____

OTRAS COSAS IMPORTANTES

_____

_____

_____

_____

_____

7 ARRIVAL

PERSPECTIVA

After weeks of preparation, your actual homestay adventure begins. This Element prepares you for arrival and meeting your host family. You learn to greet people and make introductions in Spanish. In addition, you become an international traveler who understands arrival times, international time zone changes, and airport procedures. **¿Listos? ¡Vámonos!**

CIUDAD	VUELO		HORA
LOS ANGELES	DELTA	901	2:00
HOUSTON	DELTA	283	5:00
NEW YORK	DELTA	606	9:00
RIO DE JANEIRO	AIR APLA	946	13:00
PARIS	BETA AIR	527	17:00
TORONTO	ALPHA	831	19:00
DETROIT	ALPHA	672	22:00

A. EL ITINERARIO

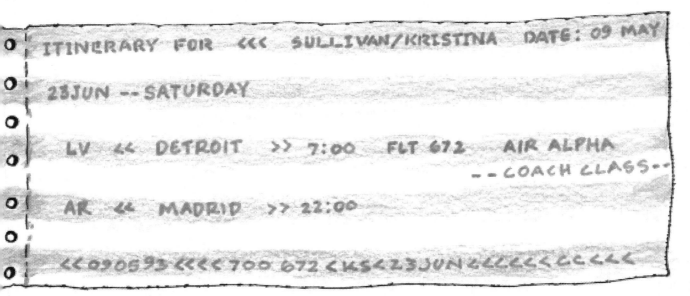

Last year, the itinerary (**el itinerario**) Kristina received from her travel agent looked like the one above. At first, she was not sure how to read the arrival time because the information was written using the 24-hour clock. When you receive your travel itinerary, you'll need to know how to interpret 24-hour time. You want to be on time for your flight, and you'll need to let your host family know exactly when you are arriving. The 24-hour clock is frequently used by airlines to indicate arrival and departure times. It's not hard to understand 24-hour time when you know the system.

Using the 24-hour clock avoids possible confusion between A.M. and P.M. In Europe and many parts of the world, it is used in schedules and timetables. When speaking, however, people normally use the 12-hour way of expressing time.

Understanding 24-hour time: In the 24-hour system, the hours for 1:00 A.M. to 12:00 P.M. are the same as they are in the 12-hour system. For hours later than 12:00 P.M., subtract 12 hours from the time to find out the corresponding P.M. time. For example, here's how to figure out what time **14:00** would be:

14:00 – 12 hours = 2:00 P.M.

Midnight is written as **0:00**.

Ready for some practice? **¡Vamos a practicar!**

13:00 _____   20:00 _____

16:00 _____   21:00 _____

19:00 _____   0:00 _____

B. INFORMACIÓN DEL VUELO

Read this **información del vuelo** (*flight information*) for the trip to your homestay country. Pay careful attention to the flight number and to the departure and arrival times.

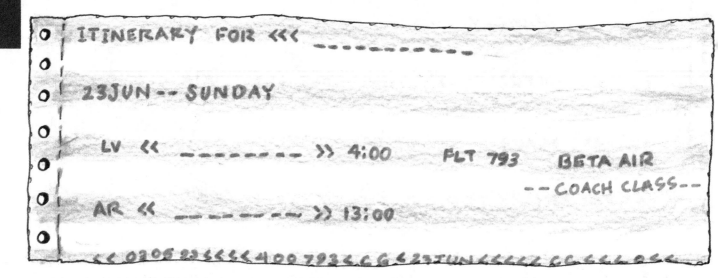

ITINERARY FOR <<< - - - - - - - - - -

23JUN -- SUNDAY

LV << - - - - - - - - >> 4:00   FLT 793   BETA AIR
                                        -- COACH CLASS --

AR << - - - - - - - - >> 13:00

<< 0205 22 <<<< 400 793 < C G < 23JUN <<<< C G <<< 0 <<

You need to remind your host family about when to meet you at the airport (**al aeropuerto**). A postcard (**una tarjeta postal**) is a quick way to tell them when your flight (**tu vuelo**) is arriving. Complete the following **tarjeta postal** with the information from your travel itinerary. Use the **dirección** for your host family that you learned in Element 5.

The Spanish word **llego** means *I'm arriving*.

Hola,
Mi vuelo es el Beta Air número _____.
Llego al aeropuerto el
_____ a
         fecha

las _____.
    hora

Hasta junio,

_____
  firma (signature)

sello
de
correo

TU RELOJ

In Element 4 you learned about telling time, and your teacher may have talked about time zones. When you travel from coast to coast in the United States or overseas, you pass through different time zones. Now that you're ready for your trip, you need to understand how time zone changes work. Remember to change your watch (**tu reloj**) to show the local time in your homestay country. You can make this change during your flight or when you arrive at your destination.

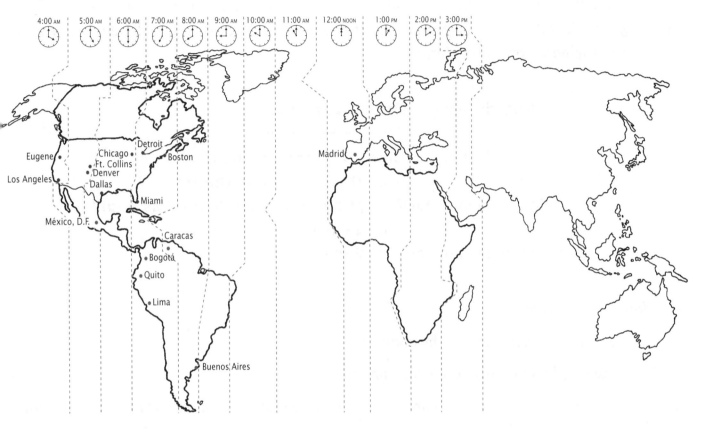

Using the time zone map above, calculate the time changes that occur when you travel between the cities listed below. Each time in the middle column shows the time in the city of departure. In the third column, write the correct local arrival time.

From _____ to _____	When you arrive, your watch says	You need to change your watch to say
1. Boston to Lima	5:00 A.M.	_____
2. Los Angeles to Caracas	8:00 A.M.	_____
3. Denver to Quito	11:00 A.M.	_____
4. Dallas to Buenos Aires	12:00 A.M.	_____
5. Chicago to Bogotá	4:00 A.M.	_____
6. Los Angeles to Madrid	7:00 A.M.	_____

D. INMIGRACIÓN: CONTROL DE PASAPORTES

When you arrive at the airport in your homestay country, your plane will land at the international terminal. First, you must pass through customs and immigration. At **inmigración** your passport is checked and stamped.

As you pass through **inmigración** you are greeted in Spanish. You are also asked some simple questions about where you come from and how long you plan to stay in the homestay country. To get ready, read the following conversation quietly to yourself. Your teacher will help you with the meanings of the new words and phrases.

Oficial de inmigración:	**Buenos días.**
Tú:	**Buenos días.**
Oficial de inmigración:	**¿De dónde vienes?**
Tú:	**De los Estados Unidos.**
Oficial de inmigración:	**¿Cúanto tiempo te quedas aquí?**
Tú:	**21 días.**
Oficial de inmigración:	**Pasa.**

Now follow these steps:

1. Listen as your teacher presents the conversation.

2. Then listen again and repeat the words and phrases.

3. Next, your teacher will read the part of the **oficial de inmigración**. Answer by reading your role.

4. Finally, working with a partner, practice the conversation several times. Take turns being the official.

5. Are you ready to go through **inmigración**? **¡Vámonos!**

After going through **inmigración**, you will meet your host family in the arrival area. To prepare for this meeting, listen to the following conversation between Kristina and the Carmonas. Making a recording of this conversation was one way Kristina kept some memories of her visit. Listen carefully! You can use these same greetings when you meet your host family.

PALABRAS NUEVAS

Bienvenida. Welcome.
Mucho gusto en conocerte. Nice to meet you.
El gusto es mío. The pleasure is mine. / It's my pleasure.
Yo soy... I am . . .

¿Cómo fue el viaje? How was the trip?
Bien. Fine.
Pero But
Estoy un poco cansada. I'm a little tired.

F. SALUDOS

The conversation in Activity E on page 77 introduced you to several greetings (**saludos**) and new expressions in Spanish. These expressions are useful when meeting people in Spanish-speaking countries. Working with a partner, practice each of the four short dialogues, changing roles each time.

Now form groups of five students and practice the entire conversation (all 4 dialogues). Each of you should take one of the roles: father, mother, Margarita, Enrique, and Kristina. Practice introducing yourselves to each other. Change roles after each conversation.

G. PRÁCTICA

For more practice (**práctica**), and to help you remember the Spanish expressions used for meeting and greeting, complete the following activity. Write the letter of the Spanish expression in the blank next to the English meaning.

1. _____ Nice to meet you.

2. _____ How was the trip?

3. _____ Welcome.

4. _____ I'm a little tired.

5. _____ My name is . . .

6. _____ It's my pleasure.

7. _____ I am (I'm) . . .

a. **Bienvenido.**

b. **Me llamo…**

c. **Mucho gusto en conocerte.**

d. **El gusto es mío.**

e. **Estoy un poco cansada.**

f. **Yo soy…**

g. **¿Cómo fue el viaje?**

I. ¡MI MALETA NO ESTÁ!

After meeting your host family, you go to the baggage-claim area. All luggage (**equipaje**) is placed in this area when it comes off the planes. Inside your airline ticket folder, you'll find your baggage claim ticket with the **número de equipaje**.

Sometimes it happens. A piece of luggage ends up on the wrong airplane. Now you know why it's important to pack a few necessities in a small piece of carry-on luggage like your **mochila**. The airline will find your luggage. To help them, you need to fill out a Baggage Claim form. Complete the following form. Remember to use the **dirección** and **número de teléfono** of your host family. Look back at Element 5 if you need to check the name, address, and phone number of your host family.

EQUIPAJE PERDIDO

Apellido _____   Nombre _____

Dirección _____

Ciudad _____

Teléfono _____

Aerolínea _____   Vuelo _____

Descripción de equipaje

☐ grande   ☐ pequeño

☐ azul   ☐ negro   ☐ rojo   ☐ marrón   ☐ verde

☐ otro color _____

I. UNA LLAMADA A LOS ESTADOS UNIDOS

Your Baggage Claim form is filed. The airline will deliver the suitcase to you as soon as it is found. It's time for you and your host family to leave the airport and drive to their home. Before leaving the airport, you want to make a phone call to the United States (**una llamada a los Estados Unidos**) to let your own family know that you have arrived safely. Remember that the times will be different between your homestay country and your hometown in the United States. Is this a good time to make a call? Let's practice a bit with time zones before you decide. Look at the time zone map on page 75 and complete the following chart. The first one is done for you.

Homestay City, Country	Time	U.S.A. City, State	U.S.A. Time
1. Toledo, España	3:00 P.M.	Detroit, Michigan	9:00 A.M.
2. México, D.F., México	6:00 A.M.	Ft. Collins, Colorado	_____
3. Lima, Perú	1:00 P.M.	Eugene, Oregon	_____
4. Caracas, Venezuela	11:00 A.M.	Dallas, Texas	_____

Now complete the chart with your own personal information:

My Homestay Country	Time	My U.S.A. City, State	Time at Home
_____	1:00 P.M.	_____	_____

Is this a good time to call? _____

MI DIARIO

You received a call from the baggage claim attendant that your suitcase has been located. The airline is going to deliver it later today. Remember to tip the delivery person when the luggage arrives. What a busy day! Think of all you have learned about traveling. Write this information under **Información nueva**. Select five to ten new Spanish words and phrases from this Element. Write them under **Mis palabras.** Put a drawing or picture of something you want to remember about your travels under **Mi dibujo**.

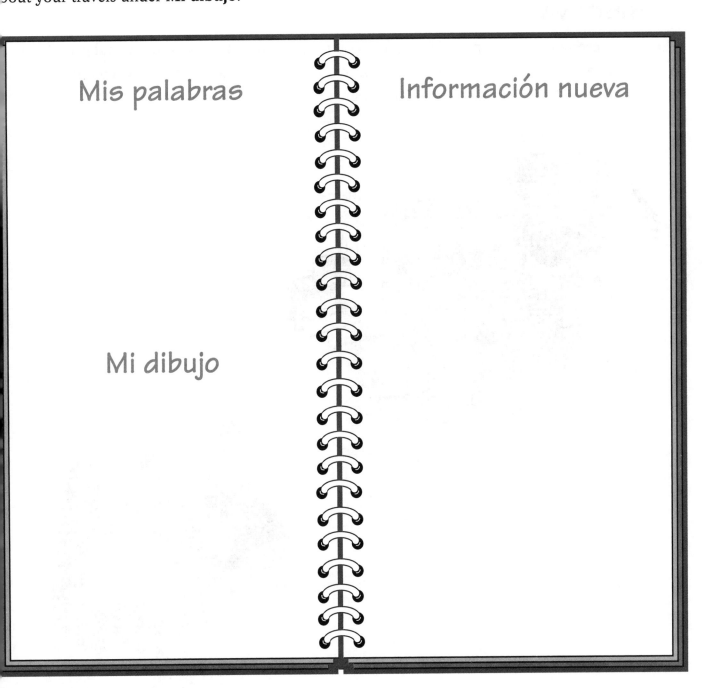

Mis palabras

Información nueva

Mi dibujo

YOUR HOMESTAY HOUSE
AND DAILY ROUTINE

PERSPECTIVA

When you arrive at your host family's house, you need to find your way around and get settled. You've had a long trip. You look forward to a snack, a rest, and getting to know your daily routin with your host family. Your homestay has begun.

A. TENGO HAMBRE

After your trip from the airport, your host mother asks if you'd like a snack. You answer politely: **Sí, gracias, ¡tengo hambre!** *(Yes, thank you, I'm hungry!)* She invites you into the kitchen to show you where you can find something to eat. To teach you how to make a typical snack, she prepares a **nacho** for you. Here's the recipe in Spanish. Does it look familiar? The first part of the recipe lists the ingredients. Do you understand the meanings of the Spanish words? Many of them are cognates or words we frequently see in the United States. The pictures will also help you understand their meanings.

nacho

pedazos de tortillas fritas

queso

jalapeños

salsa

Now you know the ingredients in a **nacho**. Here are the directions for making one. Read them twice. Read first to get a general idea of what you are supposed to do. Try to guess the meaning of any new words. Then read the directions again. This time, if you need more help, refer to the English meanings under **Palabras nuevas** in the side column.

1. Pon las tortillas en un plato.
2. Pon el queso sobre las tortillas.
3. Pon los jalapeños sobre el queso.
4. Cocina el nacho en el horno a 350°F o en la microonda hasta que se caliente.
5. Sirve el nacho con salsa.

¡Buen provecho!

PALABRAS NUEVAS

Pon Put
sobre over
Cocina Cook or Bake
hasta que se caliente
    until it's hot
Sirve Serve

¡Buen provecho! is a phrase that's often used by Spanish speakers before a meal or a snack. It's their way of saying, *"Enjoy the food!"*

Practice making the **nacho** at home. Then work with a group of your classmates. Decide how much of each ingredient you'll need to prepare a **nacho** for your class. Then make a **nacho** for everyone!

Nota The word **chile** in Spanish-speaking countries means *chili pepper*. There are many kinds of chilis, ranging from mild to very hot. They can be small, medium, or large, and they come in a variety of colors—yellow, green, and red. Some common chilis are **jalapeños, serranos**, and **habaneros**. Many Americans recognize *chili* as a stew-like dish containing tomatoes, beans, and meat. In Spanish-speaking countries, this dish is known as **chile con carne** (*chili with meat*).

Do you know of any other foods that are common in your homestay country? What are they? If you don't know any, where can you go to find out? Ask your teacher or the media center specialist to help you find this information. Then prepare a report for your class. Your report may be written or oral, or you may present visuals or a demonstration.

B. LOS CUARTOS DE LA CASA

After your snack, you are ready to learn about the house (**la casa**) where you'll be living. Look at the picture below. It shows the rooms of the house (**los cuartos de la casa**). Listen as your teacher names them in Spanish. Do any of the names sound similar to English? Could you guess which rooms your teacher was naming?

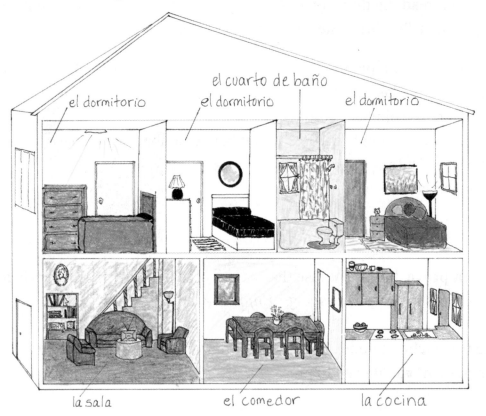

Let's take a tour **de la casa**. Your teacher will say the name of a room in Spanish. Repeat that name after your teacher as you point to the room in the picture.

C. LOS MUEBLES Y OTRAS COSAS DE LA CASA

You've had a tour of your new **casa**. Now it's time learn the Spanish words for the furnishings and other household items (**los muebles y otras cosas de la casa**). Below are pictures of **los muebles y otras cosas de la casa**. Listen while your teacher introduces the words in Spanish. Notice that the name of each item has **el** or **la** in front of it. Both are Spanish words for *the*. You learned about **el** and **la** with items of clothing and travel in Element 2.

 Nota Spanish speakers have a saying: **Mi casa es su casa** *(My house is your house)*. It's their way of welcoming you to their home. In English we sometimes say, *"Make yourself at home."*

la bañera

la cama

la cocina de gas

la ducha

el escritorio

la radio

el lavabo

la lámpara

la lámpara

la mesa

la mesa

el refrigerador

la silla

el sillón

el sofá

la televisión

la toalla

¡Vamos a practicar! Look at the pictures again. Working with a partner, take turns practicing the names of the items in Spanish. Partner A points to the picture of an item. Partner B identifies the item in Spanish. Reverse roles each time after an item is named. Then take turns pointing to all of the items, one at a time, until your partner gets one wrong. Then switch roles. Which partner is the first one to name them all correctly?

D. ¡PON LOS MUEBLES EN LOS CUARTOS!

To do this activity, you'll need pictures of furniture and other household items. You can cut these out from old magazines, catalogues, or the hand-out your teacher gives you, or you can draw your own. On the opposite page is the floor plan of **la casa**. Using this empty floor plan, **¡Pon los muebles en los cuartos!**

Follow these steps:

1. Cut out or draw pictures of furniture and other household items.
2. Place the pictures on your desk so that you can see all of them.
3. Listen as your teacher says the name of an item.
4. Place the picture of the item in the appropriate room as you repeat the name quietly to yourself.
5. Check your progress with your teacher.

Partner practice: Take turns with a partner describing the location of the item.

1. Partner A tells Partner B to put an item in a specific location. **(Pon la radio en el dormitorio.)**
2. Partner B repeats the name of the item and places its picture in the appropriate room.
3. Partner A verifies the item and its location by saying **Sí** or **No**.
4. When all of the items are positioned, change roles.

When you're sure you know the Spanish names for all the furniture and other household items, paste the pictures on the floor plan. Label each picture in Spanish.

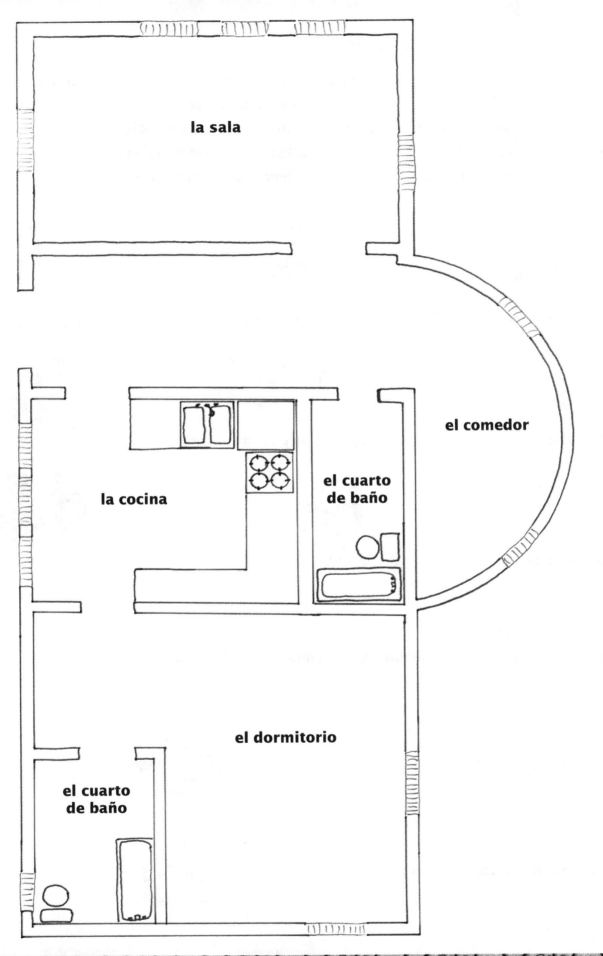

la sala

el comedor

la cocina

el cuarto
de baño

el dormitorio

el cuarto
de baño

E. UN DÍA CON ALEJANDRO

You've learned your way around **la casa** and you're beginning to feel at home. To feel more like a member of the family during your homestay, you want to follow the family routine. To do this, you need to understand and use some key phrases. Look at the pictures below. They show Alejandro doing some of his daily activities. Listen as your teacher tells in Spanish what he is doing. Next, point to each picture and repeat the Spanish sentence after your teacher.

1. Alejandro se levanta.

2. Alejandro desayuna.

3. Alejandro va a la escuela.

4. Alejandro almuerza.

5. Alejandro juega con sus amigos.

6. Alejandro hace su tarea.

7. Alejandro mira la televisión.

8. Alejandro cena.

9. Alejandro se acuesta.

¡Vamos a practicar!

Now, write the letter of each picture by the sentence that describes it.

_____ 1. Alejandro cena.

a.

_____ 2. Alejandro hace su tarea.

b.

___ 3. Alejandro almuerza. c.

___ 4. Alejandro mira la televisión. d.

___ 5. Alejandro juega al fútbol con sus amigos. e.

___ 6. Alejandro se levanta. f.

___ 7. Alejandro desayuna. g.

___ 8. Alejandro va a la escuela. h.

___ 9. Alejandro se acuesta. i.

F. ¿CUÁNDO?

You've learned the Spanish phrases to describe the activities in **un día con Alejandro**. But when (**¿Cuándo?**) does he do each activity? You already know how to say on-the-hour times in Spanish. Here are the words you need to say other times.

y	*after the hour*
y cuarto	*quarter after, quarter past,* or *15 minutes past the hour*
y media	*half past* or *30 minutes past the hour*
menos	*before the hour*
menos cuarto	*quarter to* or *15 minutes before the hour*

Here are some examples:

When?	Time	Answer
¿Cuándo?	3:05	**A las tres y cinco.**
¿Cuándo?	3:15	**A las tres y cuarto.**
¿Cuándo?	3:30	**A las tres y media.**
¿Cuándo?	3:45	**A las cuatro menos cuarto.**
¿Cuándo?	3:55	**A las cuatro menos cinco.**

Now fill in the blanks with the missing words to indicate the time shown on the clock.

¿Cuándo?

 1. a las _____

 2. a las nueve _____ diez

 3. a las nueve _____ _____

 4. a las nueve _____ veinte

 5. a las nueve _____ _____

 6. a las nueve _____ _____

. EL HORARIO DE ALEJANDRO

While you are eating dinner, your host family talks about Alejandro's schedule (**el horario de Alejandro**). After dinner, you go over his **horario** with your host mother. She gives you the specific times in **el horario de Alejandro**. Listen to the **horario** and write the times of day (using numerals) in your notebook. (Your teacher may play the role of your host mother.)

Example: You hear: **Alejandro se levanta a las seis y cuarto.**
                 You see: **Alejandro se levanta a las _____.**
                 You write: **6:15.**

Work with a partner. Read Alejandro's activities and the times you wrote in Spanish. Compare the schedules you each wrote. Verify your responses with your teacher.

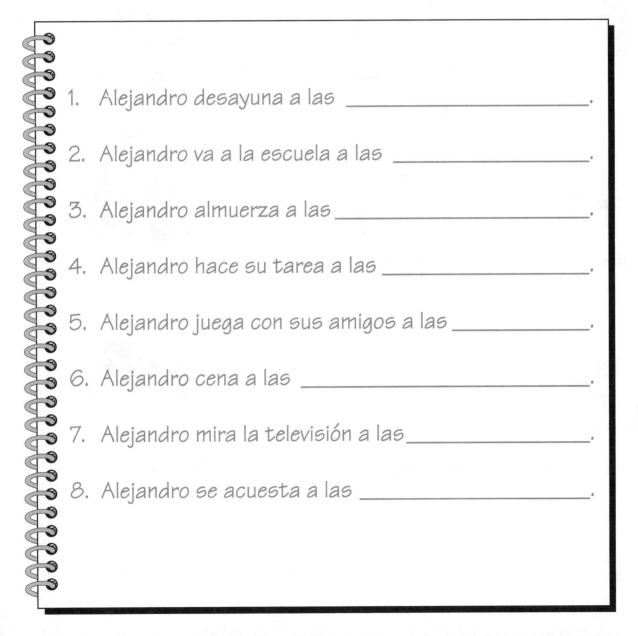

1. Alejandro desayuna a las _____.

2. Alejandro va a la escuela a las _____.

3. Alejandro almuerza a las _____.

4. Alejandro hace su tarea a las _____.

5. Alejandro juega con sus amigos a las _____.

6. Alejandro cena a las _____.

7. Alejandro mira la televisión a las_____.

8. Alejandro se acuesta a las _____.

H. TU HORARIO

Your schedule (**tu horario**) with your homestay family is very similar to Alejandro's. Look at the pictures below. These are the same activities Alejandro's mother talked about in Activity G. Now Alejandro wants to compare his schedule with yours in the United States. You need to know how to say *I* when telling him about your schedule. *I* in Spanish is **yo.** Listen as your teacher uses **yo** when describing each of the activities in the pictures. Listen again and point to each picture, repeating the phrase you use when telling Alejandro about **tu horario**.

1. Yo me levanto.

2. Yo desayuno.

3. Yo voy a la escuela.

4. Yo almuerzo.

5. Yo juego con mis amigos/
   amigas.

6. Yo hago mi tarea.

7. Yo miro la televisión.

8. Yo ceno.

9. Yo me acuesto.

Using the pictures and sentences on page 92, complete the **horario** below by telling the times of day you usually do the activities. Remember to begin each sentence with **Yo** and complete the sentence with a time of day. The first one is done for you.

1. _Yo me levanto a_
   las seis y cuarto.
   _____

2. _____
   _____
   _____

3. _____
   _____
   _____

4. _____
   _____
   _____

5. _____
   _____
   _____

6. _____
   _____
   _____

7. _____
   _____
   _____

8. _____
   _____
   _____

9. _____
   _____
   _____

I. UNA ENTREVISTA CON TUS AMIGOS

Horarios (*Schedules*) vary from country to country. They also vary from household to household. Conduct an interview with your friends (**una entrevista con tus amigos**) to find out about their schedules. Then fill in the chart below. First, show the time of day you do each of the three activities. Then show the times given to you by two of your **amigos.**

		Amigo "A"	Amigo "B"
Yo			
Yo me levanto a las _____.	Se levanta a las	_____	_____
Yo almuerzo a las _____.	Almuerza a las	_____	_____
Yo me acuesto a las _____.	Se acuesta a las	_____	_____

MI DIARIO

You have had an opportunity to learn about the daily routine in your new host family. In **tu diario**, write about your routine under **Información nueva**. Select five to ten new Spanish words or phrases from this Element. Write them under **Mis palabras.** Put a drawing of something you learned during your first day with your host family under **Mi dibujo**.

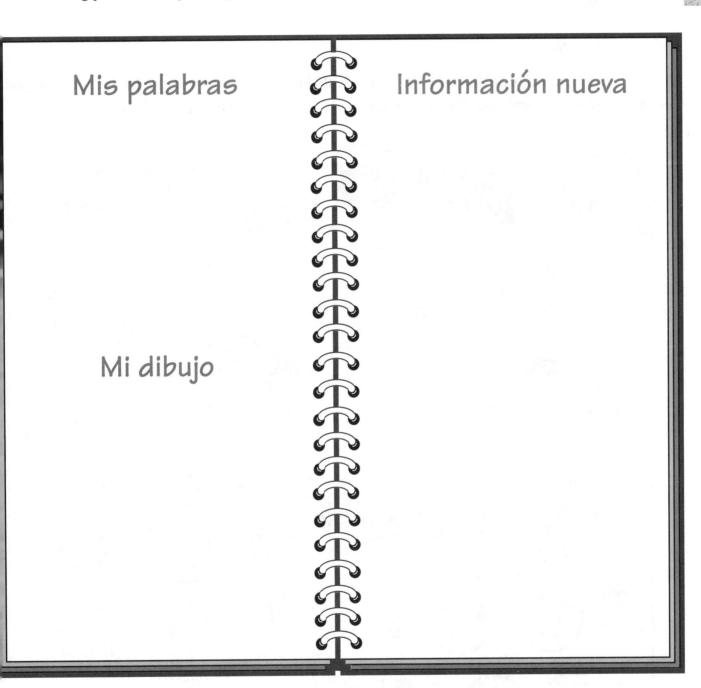

Mis palabras

Mi dibujo

Información nueva

GETTING AROUND TOWN

PERSPECTIVA

Among the most exciting attractions in a city are its local sights and cuisine. In this Element you
learn how to get around your host city and order a meal in a local restaurant.

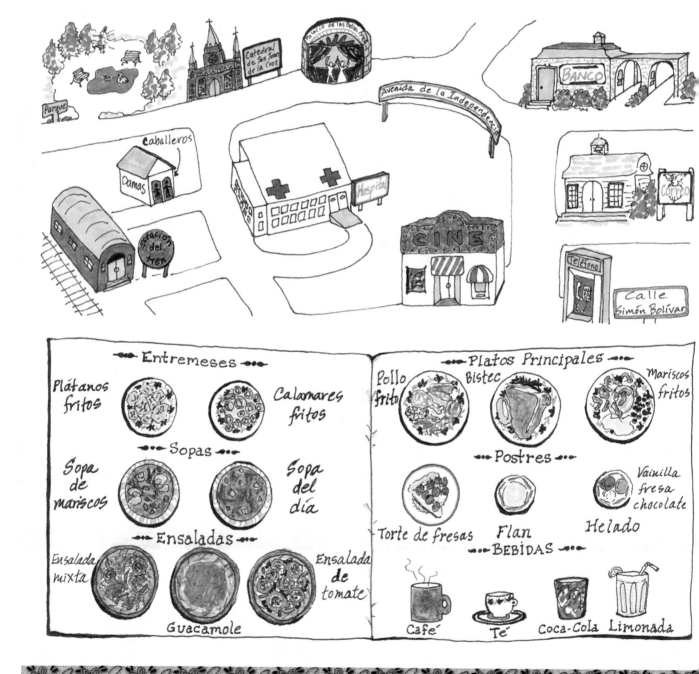

ou are excited about getting around your new city (**ciudad**). Your host family has promised to ke you sightseeing. In the meantime, you see signs (**señales**) everywhere, and you want to xplore on your own. Look at **los señales** below. Now look at the list of things to do. Which eñales would you look for to find the place where you do each of the following activities? atch each of **los señales** to the reason you would go to that place.

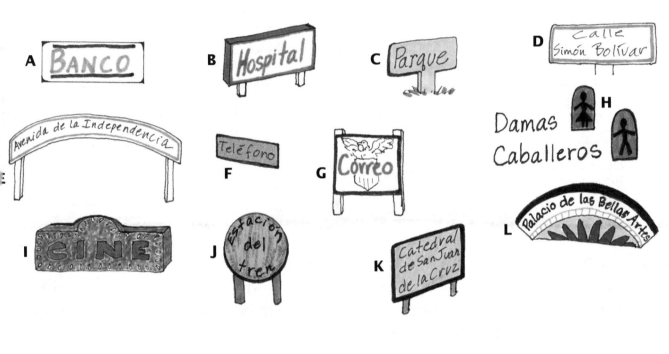

A BANCO

B Hospital

C Parque

D Calle Simón Bolívar

Avenida de la Independencia

F Teléfono

G Correo

Damas Caballeros H

I CINE

J Estación del tren

K Catedral de San Juan de la Cruz

L Palacio de las Bellas Artes

____ 1. You want to change some of your American money.

____ 2. You are going to buy some stamps.

____ 3. You want to see the main street, which is named after a very famous Spanish-speaking historical figure.

____ 4. You want to see a Spanish play.

____ 5. You want to see all the beautiful gardens.

____ 6. You need to use the restroom.

____ 7. You want to take a picture of a beautiful church.

____ 8. You want to make a telephone call.

____ 9. You would like to see a movie.

____ 10. You need to get a train schedule for an excursion.

B. FRASES CLAVES

Frases claves

1. Tengo hambre._____
_____

2. Tengo sed._____
_____

3. Estoy enfermo(a). _____
_____

4. Me perdí._____
_____

5. Necesito ayuda. _____
_____

6. Quiero una coca cola. _____
_____

7. ¿Dónde está el banco? _____
_____

8. ¿Dónde están los servicios? _____
_____

9. Por favor._____
_____

10. Gracias. _____
_____

The journal page above shows ten key phrases (**frases claves**). Look at the pictures your teacher shows you and repeat each phrase after your teacher. Now, with a partner, guess the English meaning of each **frase**. Write your prediction on the line following the phrase. Your teacher will say the phrases again. Listen and repeat them.

C. DIRECCIONES

In addition to the **frases claves** you have learned, there are some other words you need to know in order to follow directions. Listen and watch carefully while your teacher shows you some directions and positions in Spanish. Repeat them after your teacher. Then practice demonstrating them with a partner or in a small group. Do you think you can follow directions well enough now to find your way around town?

Dobla a la derecha

Dobla a la izquierda

Sigue dere●

detrás de

al lado de

en frente ●

D. EL MAPA

Here's a chance to see how well you can follow directions in Spanish. You need to go to the bank (el banco) to exchange some American dollars into local currency. Your host mother told you that there is un banco near the house. Look at the map (el mapa) of the neighborhood. Find the building labeled Mi casa. This is where you will start. Your teacher will read the directions to get to the bank. Which building is el banco? What letter represents el banco? Put that letter in this blank: _____.

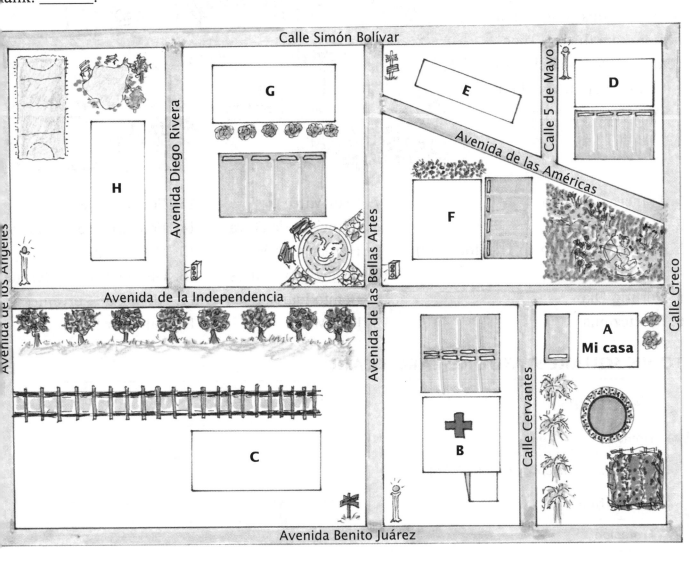

E. ¡PRACTICAMOS LAS DIRECCIONES!

Look at el mapa. Your teacher will give you directions to four different places. At the beginning of each set of directions, put your pencil on the building labeled Mi casa. This is where you will start. Listen to the directions your teacher gives you. Follow the directions with your pencil. Where are you? Write the name of the building or place in the correct box provided on the map above.

F. LA PLAZA

In the center of many Spanish-speaking cities is a town square (**la plaza**) with a statue of a famous person. Below is a list of some famous Spanish-speaking people. Choose one famous person from the list. Then complete the research card with information about him or her. Your teacher can help you.

1. Francisco Franco
2. Gabriela Mistral
3. El Greco (Domenico Theotocopuli)
4. Simón Bolívar
5. Porfirio Díaz
6. Moctezuma

7. Joan Miró
8. Francisco de Goya
9. Hernán Cortés
10. El Rey Juan Carlos
11. Benito Juárez
12. José Martí

13. Ponce de León
14. Francisco de Coronado
15. Diego Velázquez
16. Gabriel García Márquez
17. Miguel de Cervantes
18. Salvador Dalí

TOWN SQUARE STATUE RESEARCH CARD

Estatua

Nombre

Fecha de nacimiento (día/mes/año)

Ciudad/País

Profesión

Exitos y las fechas (*Accomplishments and dates*)

La historia del país durante su vida (*The history of the country during his or her lifetime*)

UNA ESTATUA DE UNA PERSONA FAMOSA

You learned that in the center of many Spanish-speaking cities, **la plaza** has a statue of a famous person (**una estatua de una persona famosa**). At the base of **la estatua**, there is often a plaque that gives information about that person.

In the picture frame below, put a drawing or other picture of the **persona famosa** you selected for your research. Use your research notes to complete the plaque.

H. EL CORREO

One of the most important buildings you need to be able to find is the post office (**el correo**). All of your family and friends back home will want postcards and letters (**cartas**). Here are some useful phrases (**frases útiles**) for the post office. Do you already know any of them? Practice thes**e** **frases útiles** with your teacher.

Buenos días	Señora Señor Señorita			
Me gustaría Quiero	enviar comprar	una tarjeta postal un aerograma un sello de correo	por avión a los Estados Unidos	por favor
Gracias				
Adiós	Señora Señor Señorita			

Hello	*Ma'am* *Sir* *Miss*			
I'd like *I want*	*to send* *to buy*	*a postcard* *an airmail letter* *a postage stamp*	*by airmail* *to the United States*	*please*
Thank you				
Good-bye	*Ma'am* *Sir* *Miss*			

 The Spanish word for *airmail letter* is **aerograma**. This word is of Greek origin. Fo**r** this reason it does not follow the usual pattern. The word ends in **-a** but uses **un**, NOT **una**.

How would you ask for a stamp to send a postcard to a friend in the United States? Working wit**h** a partner, use the **frases útiles** to create a dialogue between yourself and a postal employee.

ELEMENT

UNA TARJETA POSTAL

Below is **una tarjeta postal**. Use it to write to your family in the United States. Tell them about some of the things you're doing. Summarize what you've learned during your homestay about **la ciudad y la familia**. Then address **la tarjeta**. Don't forget **el sello de correo**!

```
sello
de
correo
```

_____

_____

_____

_____

_____

EL MENÚ

You've had a busy day exploring your new surroundings. You mailed your **tarjeta postal**. This evening, your homestay family is taking you to a restaurant (**un restaurante**) for dinner. You want to be prepared for this new experience. Can you read **el menú** on the next page? Go over it with a partner. Do you know what to order? Look for cognates, such as **ensalada** (*salad*) or **bistec** (*beefsteak*). Place a check mark (√) next to any items on the menu that are *unfamiliar* to you. Your teacher will help you understand them.

El menú

Entremeses
Plátanos fritos
Calamares fritos

Ensaladas y sopas
Ensalada mixta (tomate, lechuga, cebolla)
Ensalada de tomate
Guacamole
Consomé con limón
Sopa de mariscos
Sopa del día

Platos principales
Pollo frito
Carne de res con ajo
Paella Valenciana
Bistec
Empanadas de pollo
Lechón asado
Salmón a la parrillada
Mariscos fritos

Postres
Torta de fresas
Flan
Galletas
Torta de chocolate
Helado (vainilla, fresa, chocolate)

Bebidas
Coca cola, limonada, naranja,
   agua mineral
Café, té
Jugo de naranja, guava,
   papaya, piña

an you read **el menú**? For more practice, categorize foods from **el menú** into the columns
elow.

ENSALADA   **POLLO**   **CARNE DE RES**   **MARISCOS**

_____   _____   _____   _____

_____   _____   _____   _____

_____   _____   _____   _____

_____   _____   _____   _____

Now, decide what you would like to order for dinner (**la cena**). Circle your choices on **el menú**
n the opposite page. **¿Listos? !Vámonos al restaurante!**

K. ¿EN QUÉ PUEDO SERVIRLE?

You've decided what you'd like to eat. Do you know how to order these items in **el restaurante**?
The **camarero(a)** (*waiter/waitress*) asks: **¿En qué puedo servirle?** (*How may I help you?*) You
nswer: **Me gustaría** (*I'd like*) _____. Practice these two phrases with your teacher. Then,
vorking with a partner, practice ordering the foods you have selected on **el menú** in Activity J.
Use the dialogue below as a model.

Camarero: **¿En qué puedo servirle?**

Tú: **Me gustaría** _____ , _____ ,

_____ **y** _____ , **por favor.**

L. JUEGO DE LA CIUDAD

With some help, you've found **el correo**, **el banco**, and some other places in **la ciudad**. Let's see i
you can find your way around **la ciudad** to do things on your own. Choose a team of two to four
classmates to play this city game (**juego de la ciudad**). Here's how you play: Your teacher will giv
each team a stack of cards, a copy of the game board, colored tokens, and a die. The object of the
game is to reach the **Casa de helados** with as few cards as possible. Follow these directions carefully. The picture on the game board tells you what you find in the **Casa de helados**.

1. Each player:
   - selects a colored token as his or her own.
   - places his or her token at the start, marked **Empieza aquí** (*Begin here*).
   - draws six cards with pictures of things to see or buy.
   - rolls the die to see who goes first. (The lowest number goes first. If it's a
     tie, then those players roll again.)

2. Player 1 rolls the die and moves his or her token the number of spaces
   indicated.

3. If Player 1 lands on a space that matches a shop or place of interest shown
   on one of the cards in his or her hand, Player 1 discards that card to a throw-
   away pile.

4. If none of Player 1's cards matches the space, he or she must draw another card.

5. Play then passes to Player 2.

6. The game continues until one player reaches the **Casa de helados** and is
   declared the winner.

Here's some more information to help you play. Your teacher will practice these phrases with you
before you start. These are also **frases útiles** when you're playing other games:

2 espacios atrás	Back 2 spaces
2 espacios adelante	Ahead 2 spaces
Pierde tu turno	Lose your turn
Tira otra vez	Roll again

M. MI DIARIO

ou've learned about your host city. Did you enjoy your meal at the restaurant? In your journal, rite anything you'd like about your experiences under **Información nueva**. You may also want o include information you learned about a famous Spanish-speaking person. Select five to ten ew Spanish words or phrases from this Element. Write them under **Mis palabras.** Under **Mi ibujo**, put a photo or drawing of the famous person you studied, something you saw in the city, r your favorite food from your dinner at the restaurant.

Mis palabras

Información nueva

Mi dibujo

GOING TO SCHOOL IN YOUR HOMESTAY COUNTRY

PERSPECTIVA

Attending school and participating in extracurricular activities helps homestay students understand life in their homestay country. In this Element, you get acquainted with your new school and decide which clubs you want to join. In addition, you have an opportunity to describe your hometown school to your new classmates. **¡Vámonos!**

Nombre _____

Horario escolar: Clase 7B

Horas	lunes	martes	miércoles	jueves	viernes
9:00	el inglés	la música	el español	la historia	la informática
10:00	la historia	la informática	las ciencias	las matemáticas	el inglés
11:00	las matemáticas	el inglés	la ed. física	el español	la geografía
12:00	ALMUERZO	ALMUERZO	ALMUERZO	ALMUERZO	
13:00	el español	la geografía	la informática	las ciencias	las matemáticas
14:00	las ciencias	las matemáticas	el inglés	la ed. artística	el español

Año _____   División _____   Alumno _____

Clubes — Día

club internacional — lunes

fotografía — martes

tenis — miércoles

pintura — jueves

Preferencias

1° tenis

2° club internacional

3° pintura

4° fotografía

. LAS MATERIAS

During your homestay, you attend classes (**las clases**) with your host brother and sister. What are the subjects (**las materias**) you can select? Here is a list of **las materias** available to you in your homestay school. Listen carefully while your teacher says them in Spanish. Can you guess what they are in English? Practice repeating the names of **las materias** after your teacher. Then write the English equivalents in the blanks. Notice that the Spanish word for *the* appears in front of each subject, and also notice that the subject names are not capitalized.

Example:

el inglés   *English*

1. la música   _____

2. la geografía   _____

3. la historia   _____

4. el francés   _____

5. las matemáticas   _____

6. la educación física _____

7. la educación artística _____

8. el español   _____

9. la ciencia   _____

10. la informática   _____

 In some Spanish-speaking countries the term **asignaturas** is used instead of **materias**.

B. LOS CLUBES

Students in the Spanish-speaking world normally do not participate in organized school sports a
we do in the United States. Instead, they participate in clubs (**los clubes**), which are scheduled
late in the school day. During your homestay you may also participate in these clubs. Look at the
list below. Do you have any of these extracurricular activities or clubs in your school? If so, circl
the names of the clubs you have. Now, practice saying all the names with your teacher. Then wri
the English equivalents in the blanks. (Remember, you do not use *the* in English.)

Example:

    la pintura   *painting*

1. la natación   _____

2. el debate   _____

3. la fotografía   _____

4. el ciclismo   _____

5. el tenis   _____

6. el drama   _____

7. el volibol   _____

8. el club internacional   _____

9. los astronautas jóvenes   _____

10. la gimnasia   _____

 Nota   Drama is of Greek origin. For this reason it does not follow the usual pattern. You
say **el drama**, NOT **la drama**. In Element 9 you learned another word like this: *an
airmail letter* (**un aerograma**). The word ends in **-a** but uses **un**, NOT **una**.

MIS PREFERENCIAS

ow that you know something about the clubs and activities in your homestay school, you can
gister to participate. Below is a registration form. Complete the top part with your personal
formation. (Remember to use your homestay **dirección** and **teléfono**.) Then look at the list of
ubs. Select four and list them in the order of your preference. All of the **clubes** meet at 4:00 P.M.
rite the name of the club and the day it meets on the appropriate line.

SOLICITUD PARA LOS CLUBES

Nombre _____

Dirección _____

_____

Teléfono _____

Edad (¿Cuántos años tienes?) _____

Año escolar _____

Club	Día	Club	Día
la natación	lunes	el drama	miércoles
el debate	lunes	el volibol	jueves
la fotografía	martes	el club internacional	jueves
el ciclismo	martes	los astronautas jóvenes	viernes
el tenis	miércoles	la gimnasia	sabádo

Mis preferencias

1° _____

2° _____

3° _____

4° _____

Nota   Spanish uses a small circle after the number to indicate rank order. In English, we
use the following numerical abbreviations: 1st, 2nd, 3rd, 4th, etc.

D. EL HORARIO

You've selected your extracurricular activities. Now it's time to complete your schedule.
Review the classes and clubs available at your host school, as shown on pages 109 and 110. List
the classes you want to take in the appropriate blanks on the schedule below. Indicate the clubs
you decided to join in the blanks following **Clubes**.

Nombre _____ Horario escolar: Clase _____

Horas	lunes	martes	miércoles	jueves	viernes
9:00					
10:00					
11:00					
12:00					
13:00					
14:00					

Año _____ División _____ Alumno _____

Clubes   1° _____

2° _____

3° _____

4° _____

PAPEL, LÁPIZ Y LIBRO

Now that you have chosen the classes you want to take during your homestay, you need to buy some school supplies. In many parts of the world, students buy items such as paper and pencil (**el papel y el lápiz**) or books (**los libros**) in a bookstore (**una librería**) or a stationery and paper supply store (**una papelería**). Is this different where you live? Discuss the differences, if any, with your teacher and classmates.

_____ 1. un cuaderno

_____ 2. un lápiz

_____ 3. un bolígrafo

_____ 4. un libro

_____ 5. una hoja de papel

_____ 6. un sacapuntas

_____ 7. una regla

_____ 8. una mochila

_____ 9. una calculadora

_____ 10. una goma

_____ 11. un marcador

_____ 12. un cartelón

Here's a list of some basic school supplies. Listen as your teacher pronounces the words in Spanish. Then repeat them. Try to guess the meanings of the words. Verify your predictions with your teacher. Do the meanings of some of the words surprise you? Do you have any of the same items at home? Which ones?

List them here: _____

Working with a partner, review the words listed above and match them to the objects in the classroom picture. Write the letter of each picture by the appropriate Spanish word. Notice that each object uses **un** or **una**. You learned about these words in Element 2. When you are finished, check with your teacher to see how well you have done.

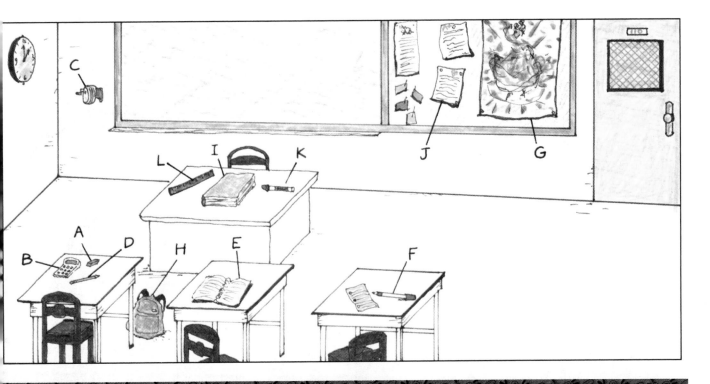

F. PRÁCTICA

Here are some scrambled Spanish words for school subjects and school supplies. Working with a partner, see how quickly you can unscramble the words. After you have unscrambled each one, write it in the first blank. Then write the letter of each picture in the second blank after the appropriate word.

1. TSAMTICEAMA _____ _____

2. BLOIR _____ _____

3. NCIECAI _____ _____

4. OGGAÍERFA _____ _____

5. ZALPI _____ _____

F $3x + 5 = 29$

6. AMGO _____ _____

7. ÑAELSOP _____ _____

8. MIGNIASA _____ _____

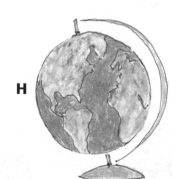

G. LAS MATERIAS Y LOS CLUBES: ¿CÚAL TE GUSTA MÁS?

Now you know the Spanish words for a number of school subjects and clubs (**las materias y los clubes**). Which ones are the most popular? Let's take a poll in Spanish. Look at the sentences below. You need to use them to take your poll. Listen to your teacher model the sentences, then repeat them. Practice them with a partner. **¿Listos?**

Questions:	**¿Qué materia te gusta más?**	*Which class to you like best?*
	¿Qué club te gusta más?	*Which club do you like best?*
Answer:	**Me gusta más _____.**	*I like _____ the best.*

Below is a list of school subjects and clubs. Use the sentences you have just learned to take a poll of 15 classmates. If your classmates do not know the Spanish phrases, you can teach them what to say. For example,

You ask:	They answer:
¿Qué materia te gusta más?	**Me gusta más la ciencia.**
¿Qué club te gusta más?	**Me gusta más el club de tenis.**

Find out each person's subject and club. Tally the results and record them on the correct line.

Las materias	**Los clubes**
_____ el inglés	_____ la natación
_____ el español	_____ el debate
_____ el francés	_____ la fotografía
_____ la historia	_____ el ciclismo
_____ la geografía	_____ el tenis
_____ las matemáticas	_____ el drama
_____ la música	_____ el volibol
_____ la ciencia	_____ el club internacional
_____ la educación física	_____ los astronautas jóvenes
_____ la educación artística	_____ la gimnasia
_____ la informatíca	

When you have completed your poll and tallied your responses, report your findings to the class. You may do this as an oral or a written report, or in a chart, graph, or any other format you select.

H. ¿CÓMO ES TU ESCUELA?

What is your school like? (¿**Cómo es tu escuela?**) You have been asked to develop a project that tells what school is like in your hometown. This project is to be presented to your Spanish-speaking classmates. Here are some instructions to help you. Read through the steps before you begin. Your teacher will give you a checklist to use as you work on the project. Check off (√) each step as you complete it. The first step has four phases. **¡Buena suerte!**

STEP 1: BRAINSTORM IDEAS AND OUTLINE YOUR PRESENTATION.

Phase 1. Working with a partner, brainstorm information you want to share about your school. What topics would be interesting to your Spanish-speaking classmates? Write all of your ideas on a sheet of paper.

Phase 2. Review your ideas for topics. Select those you want to use in your project. Write them in the cells on the idea map below. You may add more cells if you wish.

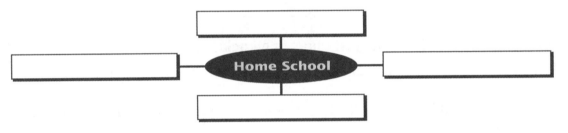

Phase 3. Next, decide on the order in which you want to present your topics. Write them in that order on the index card below. After listing the topics, discuss with your partner what specific information you want to give about each one. Then write your ideas next to the main topics on the card.

1.

2.

3.

4.

hase 4. Finally, choose the exact way you plan to present your project. You may wish to make poster and explain it or you may prefer to compose a written report. You can select any form of resentation that interests you. Your teacher will give you some other suggestions and help you ecide on the format you want to use.

Vrite the kind of project you plan to present here: _____

TEP 2: MAKE A SHOPPING LIST FOR YOUR SUPPLIES.

ook at the list of supplies on page 113. What do you need for your project? You need to go nopping (**ir de compras**) for supplies. Put them on the shopping list below. If you need items nat are not on the list, consult a Spanish-English dictionary or ask your teacher.

Las compras

_____   _____

_____   _____

_____   _____

_____   _____

TEP 3: DESIGN THE ART FOR YOUR PROJECT.

ou've planned your project and you've bought your supplies. You need to get started. Pictures, hotographs, and drawings make a project more interesting and informative. Think about how ou can illustrate each of the ideas from your idea map and index card outline. Cut out or draw ictures or use photos. Organize them on a poster, or incorporate them in another way into the resentation of your project.

TEP 4: LABEL EACH DRAWING OR PICTURE IN SPANISH.

abel each illustration using as much Spanish as you can. Remember that neither you nor your panish-speaking classmates are completely fluent in each other's language. Use simple Spanish o present your ideas. Sometimes you can use just one or two words. For example, to label a icture of your friends at lunch, you can write **amigos—el almuerzo**. You can use the word **Horario** to label a copy of your schedule and fill in the subjects in Spanish. (Refer to page 112 if ou need a reminder.)

STEP 5: PRACTICE PRESENTING YOUR PROJECT.

Practice your presentation with your partner. Your partner takes the role of your Spanish-speaking classmates. Use as much Spanish as possible. Try to be interesting and entertaining. Ask your partner for suggestions to improve your presentation.

STEP 6: PRESENT YOUR PROJECT.

Give your practiced and improved presentation to the class. Use your notes, your illustrations, and the helpful suggestions from your partner. Remember to include as much Spanish as you can

STEP 7: GRADE YOUR PROJECT.

In your host school, students may not receive the same kinds of grades (A, B, C, etc.) as you do in the United States. The grading system in many Spanish-speaking schools is from 1 to 10. (Some schools use 1 to 20 or 1 to 100.) Your project will be graded using a scale of 1 to 10. Below is your host teacher's grading scale. Can you translate the 1 to 10 scale into the grading system used in your school?

Evaluación			Equivalent in the U.S.A. System
9–10	Sobresaliente	90–100%	_____
8	Notable	80–89%	_____
7	Aprovechado	70–79%	_____
6	Aprobado	60–69%	_____
1–5	Suspenso	0–59%	_____

What do you think your grade should be for your project? _____

Why?_____

_____

Does your teacher agree? _____

Why or why not? _____

_____

I. MI DIARIO

You've had a busy time learning about the similarities and differences between your home school and your host school. In your journal, write a review of the new information you learned in this Element. Write about **tus materias y clubes** under **Información nueva**. Remember those new key words and phrases in Spanish! Write them under **Mis palabras**.

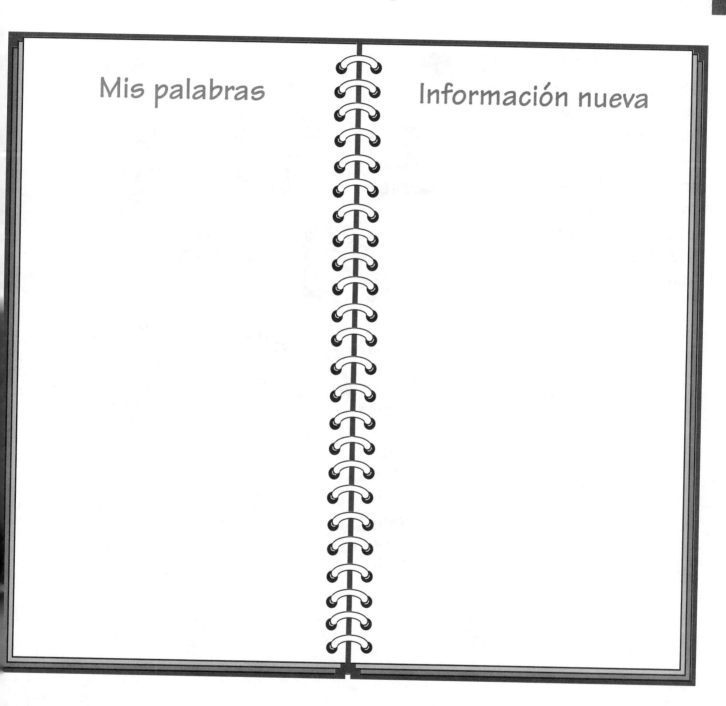

Mis palabras

Información nueva

SIGHTSEEING

PERSPECTIVA

Throughout your home-stay, you've learned about families, schools, and individual interests. In this Element you explore interesting places in the Spanish-speaking world. **¡Buen viaje!**

PUNTOS DE INTERÉS

Catedral en El Zócalo
lunes–sábado
11:00–5:00

Templo Mayor
martes–sábado
9:00–6:00

Castillo Chapultepec
martes–domingo
9:00–5:00

Museo Nacional
de Antropología
martes–sábado
9:00–7:00
domingo 10:00–6:00

Palacio de las
Bellas Artes
martes–domingo
10:30–6:30

EXCURSIONES

TOUR #1
Catedral, Templo Mayor,
Palacio de las Bellas
Artes. Sale los martes
a las 9:30 del hotel.

TOUR #2
Castillo Chapultepec,
Museo Nacional de
Antropología, Palacio
de las Bellas Artes.
Sale los jueves y los
sábados a las 8:30
del hotel.

A. PUNTOS DE INTERÉS

Travel experiences build memories for a lifetime. You will want to see as much as you can during your visit to your homestay country. There are many points of interest (**puntos de interés**) in all Spanish-speaking countries. Some of them are listed below.

Listen to your teacher and repeat the names of these **puntos de interés**. Can you guess what any of them are? Working with a partner, write your ideas and predictions in the blanks. It will be easier to predict what each one is if you look for cognates. When you are finished, verify your answers with your teacher and your classmates. Then go on to Activity B to learn more about these **puntos de interés**.

1. El Museo del Prado _____

2. El Palacio de las Bellas Artes _____

3. El Morro _____

4. El Alcázar _____

5. El Parque Chapultepec _____

6. Machu Picchu _____

7. El Museo Nacional de Antropología _____

8. El Parque del Retiro _____

9. La Alhambra _____

10. La Quebrada _____

11. Chichén Itzá _____

12. Lago Titicaca _____

13. Los Pirineos _____

14. El Volcán Poás _____

15. El Zócalo _____

B. ¿DÓNDE ESTÁN LOS PUNTOS DE INTERÉS?

Where are they? (¿**Dónde están?**) The special sites of interest in Activity A are located in several Spanish-speaking countries. Their exact locations can be found in a number of different ways. Work alone or with a partner. Choose any two of **los puntos de interés**. Find their location, history, and significance to the country. Consult sources such as encyclopedias, atlases, computer databases, or other references. Ask the librarian, media center specialist, your teachers, or others to help you. You may wish to call or visit a local travel agent for information. After doing your research, prepare a report about the two places you selected. The report may be written, oral, or visual. Use your own ideas, special talent, and imagination!

On the card below, write the names of several sites that your classmates described in their reports. Include some information you would like to remember about each of them.

Puntos de interés

Mexico City, Mexico

Machu Picchu, Peru

Cuzco, Peru

Toledo, Spain

MODOS DE TRANSPORTACIÓN

You've discovered some **puntos de interés** and want to visit one of them. To take a tour (**una excursión**), you can use different methods of transportation (**modos de transportación**). Listen while your teacher says the **modos de transportación** in Spanish and then asks you to repeat them. It's easy to guess what they mean in English, isn't it?

la motocicleta   el autobús   el metro   el auto   el tren

You may also want to walk (**caminar**). Listen again as your teacher says the words. Then practice them with a partner. Now you know **los modos de transportación**. **¡Vámonos!**

Nota In many Spanish-speaking countries the cost of owning and operating a private automobile is very high. People are much more likely to walk, use bikes or motorbikes, or use public transportation.

What form of transportation is the most popular? Working with a partner, conduct **una encuesta**. Ask ten of your classmates to tell you their 1° (**primero**) and 2° (**segundo**) choice of transportation. Each time a person answers, put 1° or 2° following the **modo de transportación**. When you're finished with **la encuesta**, report your findings to your teacher and your classmates.

Classmate	1	2	3	4	5	6	7	8	9	10
Los modos de transportación										
la motocicleta	☐	☐	☐	☐	☐	☐	☐	☐	☐	☐
el autobús	☐	☐	☐	☐	☐	☐	☐	☐	☐	☐
el metro	☐	☐	☐	☐	☐	☐	☐	☐	☐	☐
el auto	☐	☐	☐	☐	☐	☐	☐	☐	☐	☐
el tren	☐	☐	☐	☐	☐	☐	☐	☐	☐	☐

Totals:

la motocicleta	1° _____	2° _____	el autobús	1° _____	2° _____
el metro	1° _____	2° _____	el auto	1° _____	2° _____
el tren	1° _____	2° _____			

D. ¿EL METRO? ¿QUÉ ES?

What is the subway? (¿**Qué es el metro?**) If you go sightseeing in a large city (**una ciudad grande**) such as Mexico City or Madrid, you'll probably take **el metro**. Each of the following sentences has Spanish words in bold print. These are important words (**palabras importantes**) when you take **el metro**. Can you guess what these **palabras importantes** mean in English? Read the sentences quietly to yourself. Now, as your teacher reads each sentence aloud, write your prediction of the English meaning in the blank following the Spanish term.

1. You begin by going through **la entrada** (_____).

2. In order to ride **el metro** (_____) you need to buy **un billete** (_____)

3. You buy **tu billete** (_____) at a place called **una taquilla** (_____)

4. Metro lines or routes are color-coded and named for the final stop at the end of the line. That
    is your **dirección** (_____).
    (HINT: In this sentence, **dirección** does not mean *address*, it's a cognate!)

5. If you need to change lines along the way, you make **una correspondencia** (_____).
    (HINT: In this sentence, **correspondencia** isn't a cognate!)

6. The **estaciónes de metro** (_____) are named for major sites or famous people

7. When you arrive at your **estación** (_____), get off the metro, look for the
    signs, and leave through **la salida** (_____).

8. Once you pass through **una salida** (_____), you need a new **billete**
    (_____) to reenter.

Your teacher will read the sentences again to verify the responses with you and your classmates.

How did you do? Check (√) one.   **Bien** ____   **Así así** ____   **Mal** ____

Nota | Helpful hint for riding the metro: Route maps (**los planes del metro** or **los mapas del metro**) are posted throughout the cars and in the stations.

UNA EXCURSIÓN EN EL METRO

ow you have the information you need to ride **el metro**. **¡Vámonos!** On this page and the next
e some of **las estaciones** on the Mexico City and Madrid metro systems. Do you remember
eing these names before?

exico City: Moctezuma, Bellas Artes, Zócalo, Chapultepec, Zapata
adrid: Goya, Velázquez, Retiro, Colón

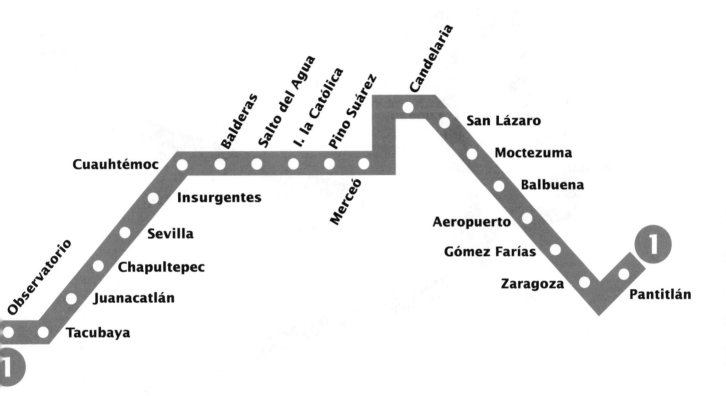

ook at the Mexico City Subway line #1. Review the names of **las estaciones**. Some names are
panish and some are Aztec. The Aztecs are an *indigenous* people of central Mexico. Can you
uess which names might be of Aztec origin? What does *indigenous* mean in English? _____
et's travel around **la ciudad en el metro**. Here are your directions. **¡Buena suerte!**

ou are at metro stop **Tacubaya** on Subway line #1. You need to go to metro stop **Moctezuma**.

1. Do you need to find **una correspondencia**? **¿Sí o no?** _____

2. Are you traveling toward **dirección Observatorio** or **Pantitlán**? Circle one.

3. How many **estaciones** do you pass? _____

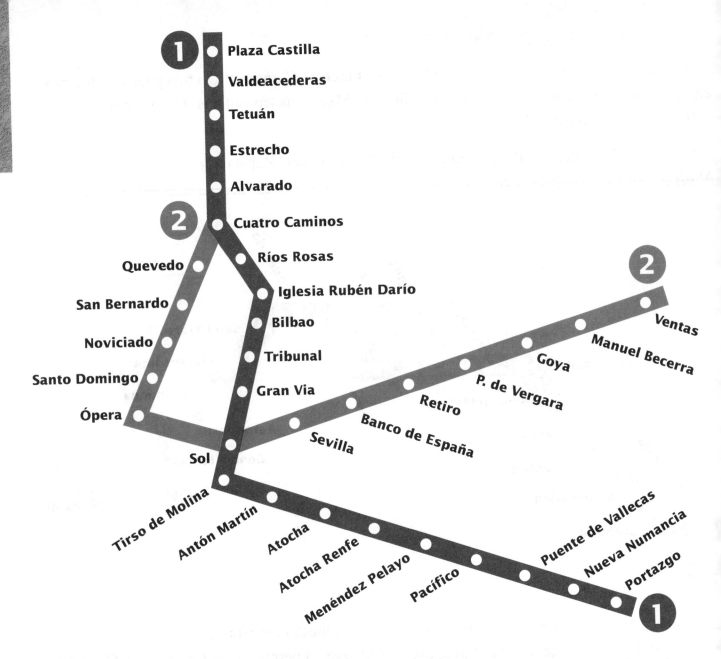

Madrid, like Mexico City, has an elaborate subway system. Look at the map and see how the Madrid metro lines connect throughout the city. Let's take **el metro** around **la ciudad de Madrid**. **¡Buena suerte!**

You are at metro stop **Pacífico**. You're going to a restaurant near **Noviciado**.

1. Do you need to find **una correspondencia? ¿Sí o no?** _____

2. Are you traveling toward **dirección Portazgo** or **Cuatro Caminos**? Circle one.

3. How many **estaciones** do you pass? _____

Congratulations! **¡Felicitaciones!** Now you can find your way around **la ciudad** like a well-seasoned traveler.

ELEMENT

F. ¿QUÉ TIEMPO HACE?

What's the weather like? (**¿Qué tiempo hace?**) The weather is an important factor when planning **una excursión**. Look at the following pictures. Each one depicts a certain kind of weather. Below each picture is the Spanish expression you use to describe that kind of weather. Listen and repeat each expression after your teacher.

Hace sol.

Está lloviendo.

Hace viento.

Está nublado.

Hace frío.

Hace calor.

Next, practice these expressions with a partner. Now your teacher will say one of them. Listen and point to the picture that illustrates the kind of weather your teacher is describing. Finally, complete the sentence below with a Spanish expression for weather:

Mi día favorito es cuando (*My favorite day is when*) _____

_____.

Why is this your favorite kind of weather? _____

_____

_____

G. UNA COMPARACIÓN DE TEMPERATURAS

Frequently, we like the weather because we like the temperature (**la temperatura**). In the United States we measure **la temperatura** in Fahrenheit degrees. Your homestay country measures **la temperatura** on the Celsius scale. Look at the thermometer on this page. It shows a quick way to understand Celsius and compare it to Fahrenheit.

Here are some average monthly temperatures for your homestay city. They are given in Celsius. Using the thermometer to help you, change the Celsius temperatures into approximate Fahrenheit temperatures. Write the new temperatures in the blanks. How does each temperature compare with those of your hometown in the United States? Place a check (√) next to the best response.

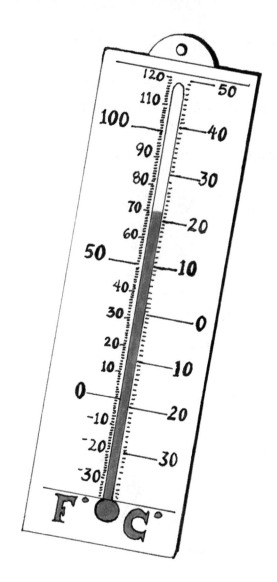

1. enero   10° C _____   Higher ____   Lower ____   About the same ____

2. marzo   24° C _____   Higher ____   Lower ____   About the same ____

3. junio   30° C _____   Higher ____   Lower ____   About the same ____

4. agosto   32° C _____   Higher ____   Lower ____   About the same ____

5. septiembre   20° C _____   Higher ____   Lower ____   About the same ____

6. noviembre   3° C _____   Higher ____   Lower ____   About the same ____

11. LAS ACTIVIDADES Y LA TEMPERATURA

La temperatura and other weather conditions often help us decide which activities to plan. Below are the Spanish words for some of the **actividades** that you can enjoy during your home-day. Can you guess the English equivalent of each? Some of them were presented in earlier elements. Working on your own or with a partner, write your predictions in English on the line under the Spanish word or phrase. Try to guess the meaning of any new words or phrases. Look for cognates. Your teacher will verify the answers with you. Then write the letter of each picture in front of the Spanish term it illustrates.

____ 1. mirar un video

   _____

____ 2. nadar

   _____

____ 3. caminar

   _____

____ 4. jugar al béisbol

   _____

____ 5. montar a caballo

   _____

____ 6. ir de compras

   _____

____ 7. ir en bicicleta al parque

   _____

____ 8. ir en canoa

   _____

____ 9. ir al cine

   _____

Now complete these sentences with three **actividades** you like to do and your **actividad favorita**:

Me gustan _____ , _____ **y** _____ .

Mi actividad favorita es _____ .

I. ¡VAMOS A PLANEAR LAS ACTIVIDADES!

You know some Spanish expressions for activities. **¡Vamos a planear las actividades!** (*We're goin to plan the activities!*) Form a group of two or three students. Below is the weather report for the week. Given these weather conditions, what kind of activities are appropriate? Decide which **actividades** your group wants to do each day. Write them on the lines following **Actividades** at th bottom of the chart . If you studied page 41 or 47 in Element 4, you learned the Spanish expressions for some other activities. You may wish to add some of those activities to this list. (If you think of other things you want to do but don't know the Spanish words, consult a dictionary or ask your teacher to help you.)

Las Actividades

DÍA	TIEMPO	TEMPERATURA	ACTIVIDADES
lunes	Está nublado.	7°C	_____
martes	Hace viento.	15°C	_____
miércoles	Está lloviendo.	26°C	_____
jueves	Hace calor.	33°C	_____
viernes	Está lloviendo.	30°C	_____
sábado	Hace sol.	35°C	_____
domingo	Hace frío.	22°C	_____

MI DIARIO

ecord what you learned about **los puntos de interés** in your journal. Using as much Spanish as u can, write about **tu excursión** and **los modos de transportación**. Write this under **Informa-ón nueva**. What do you remember about taking **el metro**? You also learned how to talk about e weather in Spanish. Select five to ten new **palabras importantes** or **frases claves** from this ement. Write them under **Mis palabras.** Draw a picture of **tu actividad favorita** or **un punto de terés** under **Mi dibujo**.

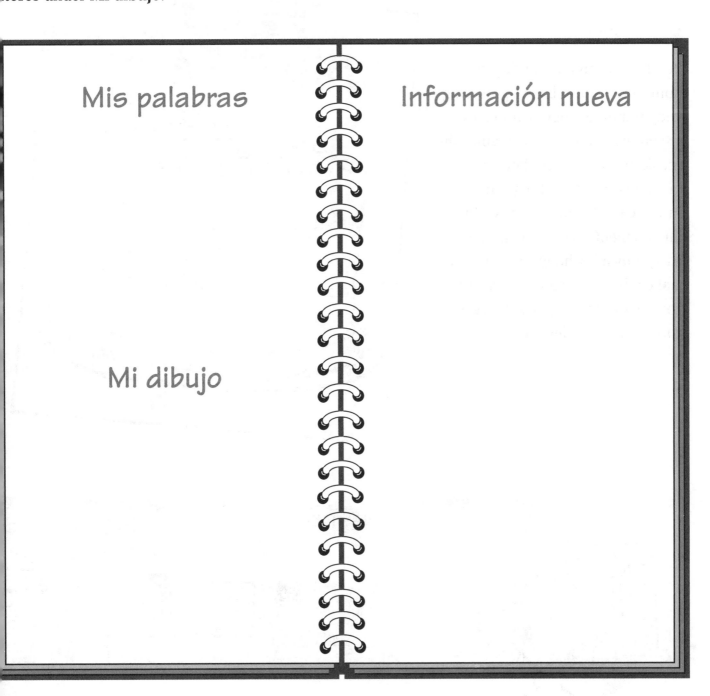

Mis palabras

Información nueva

Mi dibujo

12 A BIRTHDAY PARTY

PERSPECTIVA

You have been busy during your homestay. You've been sightseeing and attending a new school. You are enjoying meeting new Spanish-speaking friends and they have invited you to a birthday party (**una fiesta de cumpleaños**). In this Element you help plan the party, buy a birthday present, and make a birthday card. Of course, you also go to the party! Have a good time! (**¡Diviértete!**)

A. LA INVITACIÓN

Look at the invitation (**la invitación**) below. You're invited to a birthday party! Each line on the invitation begins with a word that asks a question. Can you guess the meaning of these question words in English? Your teacher will review them. Listen and repeat the words after your teacher. Then practice saying them with a partner. These words are very useful when you want to ask for information. Notice that these question words all have an accent mark in Spanish.

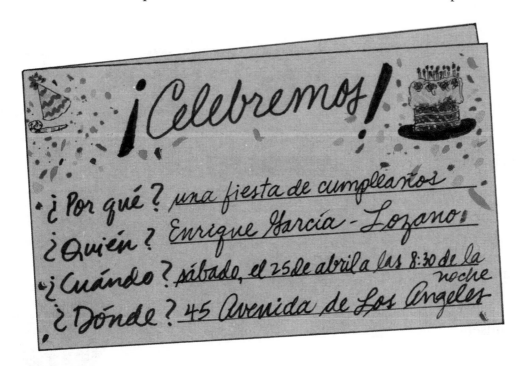

B. UNA TARJETA

You are invited to a birthday party for Enrique and are going to design a card (**una tarjeta**). Below are some Spanish phrases that are appropriate to use in a birthday card. Listen while your teacher pronounces them. Some of them have exclamation marks (**¡ !**). These phrases should be said with enthusiasm! Now listen again and repeat the phrases after your teacher.

Para mi amigo Enrique	**¡Diviértete!**
¡Feliz cumpleaños!	**¡Gozas!**
¡Que pases un cumpleaños feliz!	**Un abrazo**
¡Buena suerte!	**Con cariño**
¡Que pases un día estupendo!	**Tu amigo(a)**

Finally, decide which phrases to use on your **tarjeta** for Enrique. Your teacher will give you the materials you need to make **la tarjeta**. Plan, design, and create **una tarjeta**. When you have finished, put it in a safe place. You want to take it to the party.

C. IDEAS PARA UN REGALO

Now let's go shopping for a present! (**¡Vamos de compras por un regalo!**) Look below at the list of possible gifts (**regalos**) you could buy for Enrique. Do you know what they are in English? Work with a partner to review the items on the list. Listen and repeat them in Spanish after your teacher. Then match the letter of each picture on the right with the corresponding Spanish word on the left. When you are finished, verify your responses with your teacher.

____ 1. un disco

____ 2. un reloj

____ 3. una bicicleta

____ 4. una guitarra

____ 5. un piano

____ 6. una camiseta

____ 7. un radio

____ 8. un casete

____ 9. un juego de video

____ 10. una motocicleta

____ 11. un disco compacto

____ 12. una sudadera

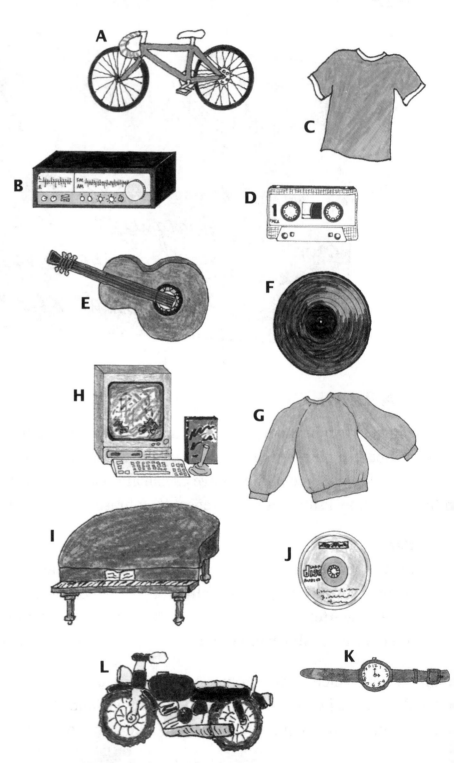

ext, on the scrap of paper below, write a list of four ideas for Enrique's **regalo**. Pretend you can
end as much money as you want. Any idea is acceptable. Be creative!

an you think of any other **regalos para Enrique**? With your classmates, brainstorm other possi-
lities. List them in the web below. If you don't know the Spanish for the choices you've made,
onsult an English-Spanish dictionary or ask your teacher. When you are finished, share your
eas with the class.

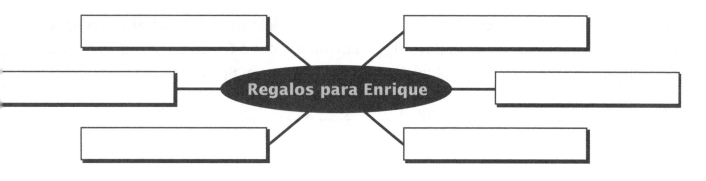

Regalos para Enrique

D. NÚMEROS PARA LAS COMPRAS

Let's go shopping! (**¡Vamos de compras!**) You want to review **los números para las compras** (*the numbers for shopping*). You've already learned to count from 1 to 100 in Spanish. Practice counting with your teacher or a partner. If you're working with a partner, take turns counting after every 10 numbers. **¿Listo? Uno, dos, tres...**

To help you with **las compras**, your teacher will dictate prices to you ranging from 1 to 100. Cross out each number as you hear it. Your teacher will give you the correct answer after dictating the number. **¿Listo?**

| 12 | 24 | 37 | 48 | 59 | 60 | 65 | 70 | 79 | 81 | 93 | 100 |

Since you have unlimited funds **para las compras**, you want to be able to say numbers greater than 100. Look at the numbers below. Listen while your teacher says them in Spanish. Do you recognize any of these numbers?

100	**cien**		800	**ochocientos**
200	**doscientos**		900	**novecientos**
300	**trescientos**		1.000	**mil**
400	**cuatrocientos**		10.000	**diez mil**
500	**quinientos**		100.000	**cien mil**
600	**seiscientos**		1.000.000	**un millón**
700	**setecientos**			

E. ¿CUÁNTO ES?

¿Cuánto es? (*How much is it?*) You're ready to buy **un regalo** for Enrique's birthday party. When you go shopping, you need to ask the price. You ask, **¿Cuánto es?** or **¿Cuánto cuesta?** Listen as your teacher asks the question. Then repeat it.

You know that Enrique likes music, and you think you might buy a CD (**un disco compacto**). Listen while your teacher asks in Spanish, *"How much does a CD cost?"* Then repeat the question. Now, write the question by filling in the missing letters in Spanish:

¿C _ _ _ _ _ _   c _ _ _ _ _ _   un d _ _ _ _   c _ _ _ _ _ _ _ _?

F. EL PRECIO

Different countries have different ways to mark prices. In Mexico they use money called **pesos** or **nuevos pesos** (**NP/N$**). **El precio** is followed by the symbol **NP/N$**. Your teacher will give you an envelope of cards representing price tags. Arrange the price tags in order from the smallest amount to the largest amount. Your teacher will say the Spanish word for a gift and then give its price. Write the Spanish term for each item on the line under the drawing and place the price tag next to it.

For example, your teacher will say:

> **Un casete cuesta cuarenta y cinco (45) nuevos pesos.**

You write **un casete** on the line under the drawing of the audiocassette and place the price tag with **45 nuevos pesos** next to it.

un casete

1.
_____

2.
_____

3.
_____

4.
_____

5.
_____

6.
_____

7.
_____

8.
_____

9.
_____

10.
_____

11.
_____

12.
_____

G. EL JUEGO DE COMPRAS

The object of the shopping game (**el juego de compras**) is to buy all the items on your shopping list and have money to spare. This is a timed activity. When the timer stops, the shopper who has found the most items on his or her list and has the most money left wins.

BANKER'S PREPARATION: (Your teacher or a student volunteer plays the role of the banker.)

1. Have available one envelope for each student (shopper) in the class.

2. Place **2.500 nuevos pesos** (NP/N$) into each envelope as follows: one 1,000 NP/N$ note, one 500 NP/N$ note, five 100 NP/N$ notes, six 50 NP/N$ notes, five 20 NP/N$ notes, eight 10 NP/N$ notes, and four 5 NP/N$ notes.

3. Give each shopper an envelope.

SHOPPER'S PREPARATION:

First, review and practice all of your numbers. Next, practice asking for what you would like to buy, saying:

Me gustaría _____ , por favor.

Then, practice asking how much any item costs by saying:

¿Cuánto es _____?
or
¿Cuánto cuesta _____?

READY FOR THE GAME? (**¿Listo para el juego?**) Follow these steps:

1. Prepare a shopping list.

   • Select any five items from the list in Activity F on page 137.

   • Write the five items on your shopping list.

   • Review the entire list to make sure you know the vocabulary.

   • Practice the words on the list with a partner.

2. From your teacher, select five cards with pictures of items on them. These will be your trading cards of items to sell. On the back of each card, write:

   • the Spanish term for the item

   • the price you are asking for the item

3. Get your money envelope from the banker.

ach shopper should have the following:

- an envelope containing **2.500 NP/N$**

- a shopping list of five items to buy

- five trading cards of items to sell

ET'S GO SHOPPING! (**¡Vamos de compras!**):

Circulate around the room asking classmates for an item on your shopping list, saying:

Me gustaría _____ **, por favor**.

If the person you approach does not have the item, he or she says either **No lo tengo** or **No la tengo**. If he or she has the item, ask how much it costs: **¿Cuánto es?** or **¿Cuánto cuesta?** The person will answer:

Cuesta _____ **pesos**.

If the price is reasonable, pay for the item with your money and take the card. If the price is too high, try to find someone else who has the same item for a lower price.

Move on to the next person, repeating the same dialogue.

When the time is up, count your purchases and your remaining cash. Be prepared to name the items you have purchased and tell, in Spanish, how much money you have left.

H. FAST FOOD

After all that shopping you realize, *"I'm hungry!"* (**¡Tengo hambre!**) Every year there are more and more fast-food restaurants throughout the Spanish-speaking world. Let's get a snack (**una merienda**)! Look at the menu. Then, get ready to order your food.

HAMBURGUESA		TÉ (CALIENTE, FRÍO)
HAMBURGUESA CON QUESO		LECHE
POLLO		JUGO DE NARANJA
FILETE DE PESCADO		COCA
PAPAS FRITAS (chico, mediano, grande)		COCA DE DIETA
CAFÉ		NARANJA

If you studied Element 9 you learned how to order food from a waiter or waitress in a formal restaurant. Fast-food restaurants are more informal. Look at the dialogue below. These are Spanish phrases (**frases**) that might be used in a fast-food restaurant. Listen and repeat them after your teacher.

hamburguesa
hamburguesa con queso
pollo
filete de pescado
papas fritas (chico, mediano, grande)
café
té (caliente, frío)
leche
jugo de naranja
coca
coca de dieta
naranja

Empleado(a): **¿Qué quieres?**

    Cliente: **Me gustaría _____ por favor.**

Empleado(a): (*Write order on form. Then repeat order aloud.*)

    Cliente: **Sí, gracias.**

      or **No, _____** (*Repeat the correct order.*), **por favor.**

Working with a partner, use the **frases** and **el menú** to practice ordering your snack. Take turns playing the role of the **cliente** and the **empleado(a)**. Remember to pronounce your order clearly.

UNA FIESTA DE CUMPLEAÑOS

You've completed your shopping for **el regalo** and stopped for **una merienda**. Your **tarjeta** is completed. It's time to plan the party (**la fiesta**). Everyone loves **una fiesta** especially a birthday party (**una fiesta de cumpleaños**). To plan the party, follow these steps:

With your class and your teacher, select:

- a party theme
- several planning committees (each responsible for planning one aspect of the party, such as invitations, food, entertainment, decorations, etc.)

Divide the class into these committees.

Each committee develops its plan. (Remember that your shopping lists, invitations, menu, etc. need to be in Spanish.)

Give each committee member a number: 1, 2, 3, 4, etc.

Send all 1's (one person per committee) to form an information group. Do the same with all 2's, all 3's, etc.

In each information group, share the plans from your original committee. Ask for suggestions, and make sure that all the plans fit together to make a great party.

Go back to your original planning committee. Share new suggestions from the information group with your original team members. Adjust your plans, if necessary.

Review your shopping lists and make your invitations. Oh! Don't forget **la piñata**!

> **Nota** **Piñatas** are made from paper maché. They can be figures of animals or other objects. They are filled with candy and party favors and are covered with decorative paper. **La piñata** is hung by a string. Each child takes a turn being blindfolded. The blindfolded child tries to break **la piñata** by swinging a stick at it. When it is broken, everyone scrambles to get the favors and the candy.

Listos? ¡Celebremos!

J. LA FIESTA PARA ENRIQUE

You're dressed for the party. Your **regalo** is wrapped. Take your camera! (You want photos for your journal.) Look again at **la invitación** in Activity A on page 133. **¿A qué hora es la fiesta?** **A las** _____. You still have time to go to the florist (**la florería**).

 It is customary to buy flowers (**flores**) for the person who is hosting a party.

As you arrive, you notice that people are talking, laughing, or dancing. Look at the picture of Enrique's **fiesta**. What do you see? To describe what you see at **la fiesta**, you say:

Veo _____.   *I see* _____.

Hay _____.   *There is/are* _____.

Work with a partner. Look at the picture. In the time your teacher gives you, identify in Spanish as many objects, people, and activities as you can. Write the Spanish words or phrases in the idea we

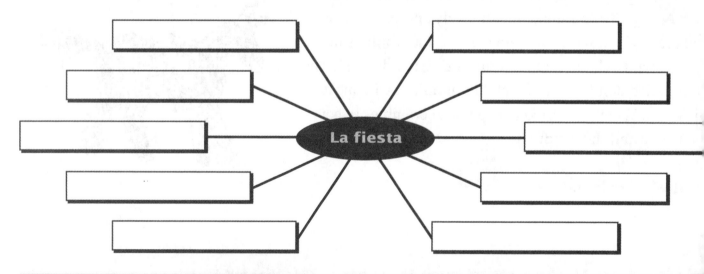

C. MI DIARIO

ou've been busy planning, shopping for, and attending Enrique's party. Write a few lines in your urnal to remember these important events. What about the gift for Enrique? Write this under **información nueva**. Select five to ten new Spanish words or **frases claves** from this Element. rite them under **Mis palabras**. Under **Mi dibujo**, include a copy of the birthday card you made.

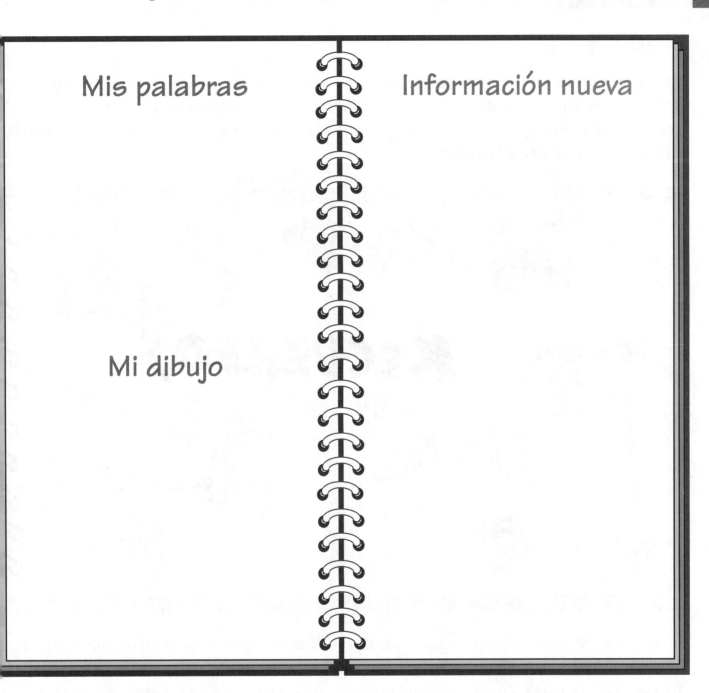

Mis palabras

Información nueva

Mi dibujo

RECUERDOS DE UN BUEN VIAJE

PERSPECTIVA

You have enjoyed your homestay experience. You met your host family and participated in their daily life. You learned about your homestay country as you attended school, rode public transportation, and went sightseeing, shopping, and to a birthday party with friends. Now it's time to go home! Too bad! (**¡Qué lástima!**)

In this Element, you construct a scrapbook of your memories (**tus recuerdos**) of your homestay experience. You want each section of the scrapbook to show a different part of your homestay. This will be nice to share with your family and friends at home! Right? (**¿Verdad?**) Your scrapbook will also help you review the Spanish you have learned. Your teacher will give you an Organization and Assessment Grid. You and your teacher will use this grid to assess your project. As you organize **Tus recuerdos** keep the criteria on the grid in mind.

. TU VIDA

ur family and friends and your Spanish teacher want to learn about your life (**tu vida**) during ur homestay. In your scrapbook, you describe the time you spent with your host family and new ends. Include things you want to remember about your new school, your favorite sites, and your tivities. Use as much Spanish as possible in your descriptions to show your teacher how much panish you've learned. Put in a lot of **fotos** and **dibujos**, too. Think about what was especially teresting during your homestay that you want to share with everyone at home. In the space low, design a cover for your scrapbook. **¿Listo? ¡Vámonos!**

B. LA FAMILIA

Your scrapbook is a perfect way to share information about your host family. Start the scrapbook by showing **la familia.** Place a picture or a drawing of them in the space labeled **La familia.** Write some information about them below the picture.

To help you begin, some sentence starters are written below. Don't limit yourself to these starter sentences, however. Be creative! There may be many things you'd like to share about **la familia** using **fotos** or **dibujos**. Be sure to label **tus fotos y dibujos en español**. If you need help, use a dictionary, or ask your classmates or your teacher.

La familia

En la familia hay _____ personas.

Se llaman _____

_____

_____

Son _____

(describe personality)

_____

_____

_____

You also want to show **la casa** where you lived. In the space labeled **La casa**, draw a picture of the house you stayed in during your homestay. Write information about **la casa** below the picture.

La casa

Mi casa es _____
(description of size and color, etc.)

Mi dirección es _____
_____

Mi número de teléfono es _____

C. MI ESCUELA

You want your family, friends, and teachers to know about your homestay school and the clubs you joined. In the space labeled **Mi horario,** include a schedule of your classes. Along with the schedule, write information about the **escuela**.

Mi horario

Mi escuela se llama _____

Mi escuela está en _____
(city)

Mis materias son _____

_____

_____

_____

_____

Include **un dibujo** or **una foto** in the space to show something about **los clubes**. Then write information about the clubs you joined.

Los clubes

Los clubes se llaman _____

_____

_____

Me gustan _____

(names of your favorite clubs)

_____

_____

D. LOS PUNTOS DE INTERÉS

You can't wait to tell everyone about **los puntos de interés** that you explored during your stay. Place a photo or a drawing of one of the sightseeing highlights in each space labeled **Punto de interés.** Write some information about each site below its picture. Give details about the history other basic information about the site. Remember to use your notes from Element 11. Use the sentence starters if you want, but don't limit yourself to them alone. You may want to include additional information about these places. If you need help, use a dictionary or ask your classmates or teacher.

Punto de interés

Se llama _____

Está en _____
(country name)

Es _____
(describe the site)

_____

_____

_____

_____

Punto de interés

Se llama _____

Está en _____

Es _____
                       (country name)

                       (describe the site)

_____

_____

_____

_____

E. LA TRANSPORTACIÓN

Your friends will be very impressed by your ability to travel independently during your homestay. This page of your scrapbook helps you tell them or show them how you were able to get around. Give some information about **el metro**. Include **un dibujo** of a subway map showing the stops. Use the **palabras importantes** you learned for traveling on **el metro**. When you describe one station, give some historical information about the famous person or location it represents.

El metro

El metro tiene _____ **estaciones.**
(number)

In order to ride a metro, you need to buy a _____.

You buy your **boleto** at a place called a _____.

When you arrive at your stop, you leave through _____.

One **estación** is named _____,
(name of famous person or location)

because _____

_____.

¡VAMOS DE COMPRAS!

our homestay also taught you that shopping in another country is different from shopping at
ome. Buying a birthday present for Enrique was a good learning experience. Your Spanish
acher and your classmates are curious about what students your age in Spanish-speaking coun-
ies buy and how much these items cost. On this page of your scrapbook include information
bout shopping. Do you still have your list of possible gifts for Enrique's birthday? Do you
member the cost of some of the items? Show **una foto** or **un dibujo de un regalo para Enrique.**
abel it in Spanish.

Es una foto (dibujo) de mi regalo para Enrique.

Una lista de compras_____

_____

_____

Mi regalo para Enrique es _____

Cuesta_____

G. INFORMACIÓN Y CONSEJO

You have learned a lot of new things during your homestay. Think about the **información** and advice (**el consejo**) you want to share with other students who are going to participate in the homestay next year. Include **dibujos**, **fotos**, and written information on this page of your scrapbook.

Información, consejo y palabras importantes

_____

_____

_____

_____

_____

_____

_____

Fotos y dibujos

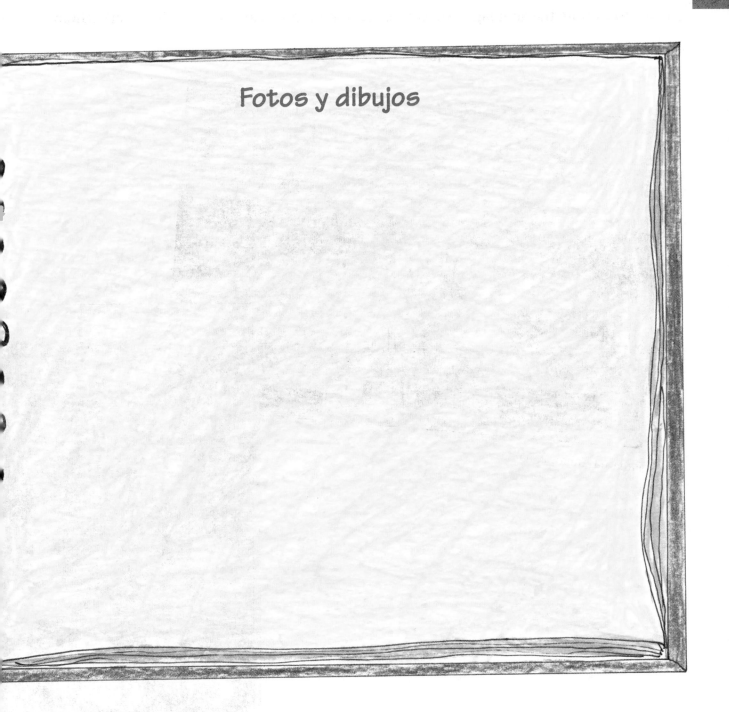

Fotos y dibujos

H. ¡BUEN VIAJE!

You are finished with your scrapbook. Now it's time to prepare for the trip back home. You have your scrapbook of **recuerdos** and some **regalos para tu familia**. Think of how much fun it will be to share your scrapbook as well as all of your experiences with your family and friends. Your classmates and teacher are sure to be impressed with all of the Spanish you know! You've had a chance to explore the language. Are you ready to continue learning more Spanish? **¡Buena suerte!**

This certainly has been a **Buen viaje**!

Panama Canal, Panama

Machu Picchu, Peru

GLOSSARY

A

at, to
a la escuela to school
a la medianoche at midnight
a las (tres) at (three) o'clock
a la una at one o'clock
a pie on foot
¿a qué hora? at what time?
brazo, el hug
bril April
ctividad, la activity
ctivo(a) active
cuesta: se acuesta (he/she) goes to bed
cuesto: yo me acuesto I go to bed
delante ahead
diós! good-bye!, so long!
erograma, el airmail letter
erolínea, la airline
eropuerto, el airport
frica Africa
fricano(a) African
gosto August
gua, el water
agua mineral, el mineral water
jo, el garlic
(a + el) to the, at the, at, by
al lado de next to
al mediodía at noon
lbúm, el album
lcázar, el palace, citadel
lmuerza (he/she) eats lunch
lmuerzo, el lunch
lmuerzo, yo I eat lunch
lumno(a), el/la pupil
marillo(a) yellow
mbicioso(a) ambitious
mérica Central Central America
mérica del Norte North America
mérica del Sur South America
mericano(a) American
miga, la friend (female)
migo, el friend (male)

anaranjado(a) orange
animal, el animal
animal doméstico domestic animal
año, el year
año escolar, el school year
¿Cuántos años tiene... ? How old is . . . ?
¿Cuántos años tienes? How old are you?
antropología, la anthropology
apartamento, el apartment
apellido, el last name
aprobado(a) approved
aprovechado(a) diligent, studious
aquí here
arrogante arrogant
arte, el art
artístico(a) artistic
asado(a) roasted, barbecued
así thus, so
así así so-so
asignatura, la subject, course (school)
astronauta, el astronaut
atrás back
auto, el car, automobile
autobús, el bus
avenida, la avenue
aviación, la aviation
avión, el airplane, plane
ayuda, la help
Necesito ayuda. I need help.
azul blue

B

bailar to dance
banco, el bank
baño, el bathtub
básquetbol, el basketball
béisbol, el baseball
bellas artes, las fine arts
bicicleta, la bicycle
bien fine; well
muy bien very well
bienvenido welcome
billete, el ticket, note, bill

biología, la biology
bistec, el beefsteak
blanco(a) white
blusa, la blouse
boleto, el ticket
bolígrafo, el pen
buen good
¡Buen provecho! Enjoy the food!
¡Buen viaje! Have a good trip!
Hace buen tiempo. The weather's nice.
¡Buena suerte! Good luck!
Buenos días. Hello.

C

caballo, el horse
café, el coffee; café
calamar, el squid
calcetines, los socks
calculadora, la calculator
caliente hot
calor, el heat
hace calor it's hot
calle, la street
cama, la bed
camarero(a) waiter/waitress
caminar to walk
camino, el path, road
camisa, la shirt
camiseta, la T-shirt
campo de tenis, el tennis court
canoa, el canoe
cansado(a) tired
estoy cansado(a) I'm tired
Caribe, el Carribean
cariño affection, care
con cariño warmly, with love
cariñoso(a) affectionate, loving
carne, la meat
carne de res con ajo beef with garlic
carta, la letter
cartelón, el posterboard, large poster
casa, la home; house
a casa at home

Mi casa es su casa. Make yourself at home.
casa de helados ice-cream stand
casete, el cassette
castillo, el castle
catedral, la cathedral
catorce fourteen
cebolla, la onion
¡Celebremos! Let's celebrate!
cena (he/she) eats dinner
cena, la dinner, supper
ceno, yo I eat dinner
central central
cepillo, el brush
cepillo de dientes toothbrush
cerca (de) near, close (to)
cero, el zero
ciclismo, el bicycling
cien one hundred
cien mil a hundred thousand
ciencia, la science
cinco five
cincocientos five hundred
cincuenta fifty
cine, el movie theater
cinturón, el belt
ciudad, la city, town
clase, la class, classroom
en clase in class
en la clase in the classroom
clave essential
cliente, el/la client, customer
club, el club
coca cola, la Coca-cola
coca de dieta diet coke
cocina (he/she) cooks, bakes
cocina, la kitchen
cocina de gas gas stove
color, el color
colorado(a) colored
comedor, el dining room
comer to eat
comer en un restaurante to eat in a restaurant
como as, like
¿cómo? how?, what?
¿Cómo es...? How is . . . ? What is . . . like?

¿Cómo es tu escuela? What is your school like?

¿Cómo fue el viaje? How was the trip?

¿Cómo se dice...? How do you say . . . ?

¿Cómo se llama? What's his/her name?

¿Cómo te llamas? What's your name?

comparación, la comparison

comparar to compare

comprar to buy

compras, las purchases

de compras shopping

ir de compras to go shopping

común common

en común in common

comunicación, la communication

con with

con mucho gusto with pleasure

concierto, el concert

consejo, el advice

consomé, el consommé

consomé con limón consommé with lemon

control, el control

cordillera, la mountain chain

correo, el post office

correspondencia, la (subway) transfer

corto(a) short

cosa, la thing

cuaderno, el notebook

cúal which

¿Cúal club te gusta más? Which club do you like best?

cuando when

¿cuándo? when?

¿cuánto(s)? how much? how many?

¿Cuánto cuesta(n)? How much does it (do they) cost?

¿Cuánto es? How much is it?

¿Cuántos años tiene... ? How old is . . . ?

¿Cuántos años tienes? How old are you?

¿Cuánto tiempo te quedas aquí? How long will you be here?

cuarenta forty

cuarto, el room

cuarto de baño bathroom

cuarto, el quarter

(son las dos) menos cuarto (it's) a quarter to (two)

(son las dos) y cuarto (it's) a quarter after (two)

cuatro four

cuatrocientos four hundred

cuerpo, el body

cuesta: ¿Cuánto cuesta(n)...? How much do(es) . . . cost?

cumpleaños, el birthday

Feliz cumpleaños. Happy birthday.

CH

chaqueta, la jacket

cheque, el check

chico(a) child

chile, el chili pepper

chile con carne chili with meat

chocolate, el (hot) chocolate

D

datos personales, los personal information

de of, from, than, in

¿De dónde...? From where . . . ?

¿De dónde vienes? Where do you come from?

de la mañana in the morning

de la noche at night, in the evening, P.M.

de la tarde in the afternoon

más de (10) more than (10)

debate, el debate, discussion

del (de + el) of the

del vuelo of the flight

deporte, el a sport

derecha, la right

desayuna (he/she) has breakfast

descripción, la description

detrás de behind

día, el day

Buenas días. Good morning.

un día de clase day in school

diario, el diary, journal

dibujo, el drawing

diccionario, el dictionary

dice: se dice you say

¿Cómo se dice...? How do you say . . . ?

diciembre December

diecinueve nineteen

dieciocho eighteen

dieciseis sixteen

diecisiete seventeen

diente, la tooth

pasta de dientes, la toothpaste

dieta, la diet

coca de dieta diet coke

diez ten

dirección, la address; direction

disco, el record

disco compacto, el compact disc

¡Diviértete! Have a good time!

división, la division

dobla:

Dobla a la derecha. Turn right.

Dobla a la izquierda. Turn left.

doce twelve

a las doce at noon

dólar, el dollar

domingo Sunday

dominóes, los dominoes

¿dónde? where?

¿De dónde...? From where . . . ?

¿Dónde está(n)... ? Where is(are) . . . ?

dormitorio, el dormitory

dos two

doscientos two hundred

drama, el play, drama

ducha, la shower

durante during

E

edad, la age

educación física, la physical education

egoísta selfish

el the

El gusto es mío. The pleasure is mine.

empanada, la meat pie

empanada de pollo chicken pie

empieza begin

Empieza aquí. Begin her

empleada, la employee (female)

empleado, el employee (male)

en in, on, by, at

en casa at home

en clase in class

en común in common

en español in Spanish

en frente de in front of

¿En qué puedo servirle? How may I help you?

en tren (auto) by train (car)

encuesta, la survey

enero January

enfermo(a) sick, ill

ensalada, la salad

entrada, la entry

entre between

entremeses, los appetizers

entrevista, la interview

entusiasmado(a) excited

enviar to send

envidioso(a) jealous

equipaje, el baggage, luggage

equipo, el team

es (he/she/it) is

Es de... (He/She) is from . . .

Es el (doce) de (julio). It (July 12).

Es medianoche. It's midnight.

Es mediodía. It's noon.

escolar of school

año escolar, el school year

escrito(a) written

escritorio, el desk

escuchar música to listen t music

escuela, la school

espacio, el space

España Spain

español, el Spanish

esperando: estoy esperando I'm waiting

espontáneo(a) spontaneous

esquí, el skiing

esquí acuático, el water skiing

está (he/she/it) is, is located

está lloviendo it's rainin;

está nublado it's cloudy

tación de metro, la subway stop, station
estación del tren train station
tados Unidos, los United States
tatua, la statue
timado(a) dear
toy I am
estoy enfermo(a) I'm sick
estoy entusiasmada I am excited
estoy esperando I'm waiting for
trecho, el strait
tudiante, el/la student
tudio I study
tupendo(a) marvelous, wonderful
iqueta, la tag, label
etiqueta de equipaje luggage tag
ropa Europe
aluación, la evaluation
cursión, la trip, excursion
ito, el accomplishment, success
trovertido(a) extroverted

F

cil easy
Fácil, ¿verdad? Easy, isn't it?
lda, la skirt
lso(a) false
milia, la family
moso(a) famous
vor: por favor please
vorito(a) favorite
brero February
cha, la date
fecha de naciemiento, la birthdate
licitaciones congratulations
liz happy
¡Feliz cumpleaños! Happy birthday!
sta, la party
fiesta de cumpleaños birthday party
ete de pescado, el fish sandwich
ma, la signature
ica, la physics
n, el custard
rería, la florist's shop
res, las flowers

formulario, el form
foto, la photo, picture
fotografía, la photograph
francés, el French
frase, la phrase, sentence
frases claves key phrases
fregadero, el sink
fresa, la strawberry
frío, el cold
hace frío it's cold
frito(a) fried
fruta, la fruit
fue was
fútbol, el soccer

G

galería, la gallery
gato, el cat
generoso(a) generous
geografía, la geography
gimnasia, la gymnastics
gobierno, el government
golfo, el gulf
goma, la eraser
gracias thank you
grande large
guitarra, la guitar
gusta(n):
les gusta(n) they like
me gusta(n) I like
me gusta(n) más I prefer
me gustaría I'd like
no me gusta(n) I don't like
gusto: El gusto es mío. The pleasure is mine.

H

hablador(a) talkative
hablar to talk, to speak
hablar con amigos to talk with friends
hablar por teléfono to talk on the phone
hacer to do, to make
hace calor it's hot
hace frío it's cold
hace sol it's sunny
hace su tarea (he/she) does his/her homework assignment
hace un viaje (he/she) goes on a trip
hace viento it's windy
¿Qué tiempo hace? What's the weather like?

hago, yo I do
hambre, la hunger
tengo hambre I'm hungry
hamburguesa, la hamburger
hamburguesa con queso cheeseburger
hasta until
hasta (junio) see you in (June)
hasta que se caliente until it's hot
hay there is, there are
helado, el ice cream
helado de vainilla, el a vanilla ice-cream
hermana, la sister
hermano, el brother
historia, la history
hoja, la sheet
hoja de papel, la sheet of paper
¡Hola! Hi!, Hello!
hora, la hour; time
¿Qué hora es? What time is it?
horario, el schedule
horno, el oven
hóspital, el hospital
hotel, el hotel

I

idea, la idea
importante important
impresión, la impression
primera impresión first impression
indeciso(a) indecisive
independiente independent
información, la information
informática, la computer science
inglés, el English
inmigración, la immigration
inteligente intelligent
interés, el interest
internacional international
invitación, la invitation
ir to go
ir al cine to go to the movies
ir al parque to go to the park
ir de compras to go shopping
ir en bicicleta to go on bicycle
ir en canoa canoeing

itinerario, el itinerary
izquierda, la left

J

jalapeño, el hot chili pepper
jeans, los jeans
jóven young
jovenes, los young people
joyería, la jewelry
juego, el game
juego de compras shopping game
juego de la ciudad city game
jueves Thursday
jugar to play
jugar al tenis to play tennis
jugo, el juice
jugo de naranja orange juice
julio July
junio June

K

karate, el karate

L

la the
lado: al lado de beside; next to
lago, el lake
lámpara, la lamp
lápiz, el pencil
las the
leche, la milk
lechón, el pork
lechuga, la lettuce
leer to read
lengua, la language
les gusta(n)... they like . . .
levanta: se levanta (he/she) gets up
levanto: yo me levanto I get up
librería, la bookstore
libro, el book
limón, el lemon
limonada, la lemonade
listo(a) ready
¿Listo para el juego? Ready for the game?
los the
lunes Monday

LL

llama(n):
  Se llama... His/Her name is . . .
  Se llaman... Their names are . . .
llamada, la phone call
llamas: ¿Cómo te llamas? What's your name?
llamo: Me llamo... My name is . . .
llego I arrive, I am arriving
llenar to fill (out)
  llenar el formulario to fill out a form
lloviendo raining
  está lloviendo it's raining

M

madre, la mother
maestra, la teacher (female)
maestro, el teacher (male)
mal bad
maleta, la suitcase
  hacer la maleta to pack a suitcase
mamá, la mom
mapa, el map
mar, el sea
  Mar Caribe Carribean Sea
  Mar Mediterráneo Mediterranean Sea
marcador, el marker
mariscos, los shrimps
marrón brown
martes Tuesday
marzo March
más more, best
  me gusta(n) más I prefer
matemáticas, las mathematics
materia, la subject
mayo May
me me, to me
  me gusta(n)... I like . . .
  me gustaron mucho I liked them a lot
  me llamo... My name is . . .
  no me gusta(n)... I don't like . . .
media, la half
mediano(a) medium; average
medianoche, la midnight
mediodía, el noon
menos minus, less; before

menos cuarto quarter to, 15 minutes before (the hour)
menú, el menu
merienda, la (afternoon) snack
mes, el month
mesa, la table
metro, el metro, subway
mi my
microonda, la microwave
miércoles Wednesday
mil thousand
millón, el million
mirar to watch
  mirar televisión to watch television
miro, yo I watch
mis my
mixto(a) mixed
mochila, la backpack
modo, el means, method
  modos de transportación methods of transportation
montar a caballo to ride a horse
monumento, el monument
motocicleta, la motorcycle
muchacha, la girl
muchacho, el boy
mucho a lot, much
  Mucho gusto en conocerte. I'm pleased to meet you.
  mucho que hacer a lot to do
mueble, el piece of furniture
museo, el museum
música, la music
muy very

N

nación, la nation
nacho, el nacho
nadar to swim
naranja, la orange soda
natación, la swimming
necesito I need
  Necesito ayuda. I need help.
negro(a) black
no no; not
  No me gusta(n)... I don't like . . .
  No te olvides Don't forget
noche, la night
  de la noche at night

nombre, el name
notable remarkable
novecientos nine hundred
noventa ninety
noviembre November
nublado cloudy
  está nublado it's cloudy
nueve nine
nuevo(a) new
número, el number

O

obediente obedient
observatorio, el observatory
océano, el ocean
  Océano Atlántico Atlantic Ocean
  Océano Pacífico Pacific Ocean
octubre October
ochenta eighty
ocho eight
ochocientos eight hundred
oficial, el clerk, official
ojo, el eye
olvidar to forget
  No te olvides Don't forget
once eleven
ópera, la opera
organización, la organization
otro(a) other, another

P

padre, el father
padres, los parents
paella, la paella
país, el country
pájaro, el bird
palabra, la word
  palabras importantes important words
palacio, el palace
pantalones, los pants
  pantalones cortos shorts
papá, el dad
papa, la potato
  papas fritas French fries
papaya, la papaya fruit
papel, el paper
papelería, la paper supply store
par, el pair
para for
paraguas, el umbrella
parque, el park

el parque zoológico zoo
partido, un match, game
  un partido de (fútbol) (soccer) game
Pasa Go ahead, Move along
pasaporte, el passport
pasta de dientes, la toothpaste
pastelería, la pastry shop
pedazo, el piece
  un pedazo de pan piece of bread
peinilla, la comb
pelo, el hair
pequeño(a) small
perder to lose
perdido(a) lost
perezoso(a) lazy
pero but
perro, el dog
persona, la person
perspectiva, la perspective
peso, el the peso
pez (pescado), el fish
  filete de pescado, el fish sandwich
piano, el piano
pie, el foot
  a pie on foot
Pierde tu turno. Lose your turn.
piña, la pineapple
piñata, la pot full of sweets
pintura, la paint, painting
Pirineos, los Pyrenees
pizza, la pizza
planear to plan
plátano, el banana
  plátanos fritos fried bananas
plato, el plate
  plato principal entree
plaza, la town square
poco, un a little
poder: poder estar to be able to be
policía, la police
pollo, el chicken
pon put
por by
  por avión by airmail
  por favor please
  por teléfono on the telephone
postre, el dessert
práctica, la practice
practicar to practice
preferencia, la preference
primero(a) first

primera impresión, la first impression

primera vez, la the first time

primero, el the first

el primero de (julio) the first of (July)

principal main, principal

privado(a) private

profesión, la profession

provecho: ¡Buen provecho! Enjoy the food!

público(a) public

punto, el point

puntos de interés points of interest

¿qué? what?

¿A qué hora? At what time?

¿Qué es...? What is . . . ?

¿Qué hora es? What time is it?

¡Qué lástima! Too bad!

¿Qué quieres? What would you like?

¿Qué tiempo hace? What's the weather like?

querido(a) dear

quedas: ¿Cuánto tiempo te quedas aquí? How long will you be here?

queso, el cheese

quiero I want, would like (to)

Quiero presentarme. I want to introduce myself.

quieto(a) quiet

quince fifteen

quinientos five hundred

radio, la radio

escuchar la radio listen to the radio

raqueta de tenis, la tennis raquet

recuerdo, el memory, souvenir

refrigerador, el refrigerator

regalo, el gift, present

regla, la ruler

reloj, el clock; wristwatch

res: carne de res, la beef

respuesta, la response, answer

restaurante, el restaurant

río, el river

rodeo, el rodeo

rojo(a) red

rosado(a) pink

sábado Saturday

sacapuntas, el pencil sharpener

sala, la living room

sale (he/she) leaves

salida, la exit, departure

salmón, el salmon

salsa, la sauce

saludo, el greeting

sándwich, el sandwich

sed, la thirst

tengo sed I'm thirsty

segundo, el the second

seis six

seiscientos six hundred

sello, el stamp

sello de correo postage stamp

semana, la week

sentimental emotional, sentimental

señales, los signs

Señor, el (Sr.) Sir (Mr.)

Señora, la (Sra.) Madam (Mrs.)

Señorita, la (Srta.) Miss

séptimo seventh

séptimo grado, el the seventh grade

septiembre September

servicio, el service

servir to help

sesenta sixty

setecientos seven hundred

setenta seventy

sí yes

siete seven

sigue follow, continue

Sigue derecho. Go straight.

silla, la chair

simpático(a) nice, friendly

sinceramente sincerely

sobre over, on, about

sobre, el envelope

sobresaliente excellent

sofá, el sofa

sol, el sun

hace sol it's sunny

solicitud, la application

son they are

son de... (they) are from . . .

son las (dos) it's (two) o'clock

sopa, la soup

sopa del día soup of the day

sopa de mariscos shellfish soup

soy I'm

soy de I'm from

su his, her, your

su vida his/her/your life, lifetime

sudadera, la sweat shirt

suerte, la luck

¡Buena suerte! Good luck!

suéter, el sweater

sur, el south

sus his, her, your

suspenso failed (in school)

taco, el taco

también also, too

taquilla, la ticket office

tarde, la afternoon

tarea, la homework, assignment

hace su tarea (he/she) does his/her homework

tarjeta, la card

tarjeta postal postcard

taxi, el taxi

té, el tea

teléfono, el telephone

llamar por teléfono to call on the phone

número de teléfono, el telephone number

televisión, la television

temperatura, la temperature

templo, el temple

tengo I have

tengo... años I am . . . years old

tengo hambre I'm hungry

tengo sed I'm thirsty

tenis, el tennis

raqueta de tenis, la tennis racket

tiempo, el weather

¿Qué tiempo hace? What's the weather like?

tienda, la shop, store

tienda de música music store

tiene(n) has (have)

el metro tiene (diez) estaciones the metro has (ten) stops

tiene... años (he/she/it) is . . . years old

tienen... años (they) are . . . years old

tímido(a) shy, timid

tira: Tira otra vez. Roll again.

toalla, la towel

todo(a) all

tomar fotografías to take pictures

tomate, el tomato

torta, la cake, tart

torta de chocolate chocolate cake

torta de fresas strawberry cake

tortilla, la tortilla

trabajador(a) hard-working

transportación, la (method of) transportation

trece thirteen

treinta thirty

treinta y uno thirty-one

tren, el train

tres three

trescientos three hundred

tu your

tú you

turno, el turn

tus your

un (una) a, an; one

uno one

útil useful

frases útiles useful phrases

va go; goes

va a la escuela go to school; (he/she) goes to school

vainilla, la vanilla

valiente courageous

¡Vámonos! Let's go!

vamos (a) we're going (to); let's go

vamos a planear... we're going to plan . . .

¡Vamos de compras! Let's go shopping!

¡Vamos de compras por un regalo! Let's go shopping for a present!

vecindad, la neighborhood

veinte twenty

veinticinco twenty-five

veinticuatro twenty-four

veintidos twenty-two

veintinueve twenty-nine

veintiocho twenty-eight

veintiseis twenty-six

veintisiete twenty-seven

veintitres twenty-three

veintiuno twenty-one

veo I see

¿Verdad? Right?

verdadero(a) true

verde green

vestido(a) dressed

vestido, el dress; costume

vez, la time, occurrence

  primera vez first time

  una vez once

viajar to travel

viaje, el trip, journey

  hacer un viaje to go on a trip

vida, la life, lifetime

video, el video

viento, el wind

  hace viento it's windy

viernes Friday

violeta violet, purple

visita, la visit

visitar to visit

volcán, el volcano

volibol, el volleyball

voy a I go (am going) to

vuelo, el flight

Y

y and

ya already

  Ya tienes... You already have . . .

yo I

Z

zapatos, los shoes